Life In The Muscle Shoals

By

Kenneth R. Johnson

Published by:
Bluewater Publications

www.BluewaterPublications.com

Preface

The Muscle Shoals area of Northwest Alabama has a long and interesting history. Unfortunately that comprehensive history has never been written. This book only partially meets the need for a history of the Muscle Shoals area.

After joining the history faculty of the University of North Alabama in 1966, I have had the opportunity to speak to civic and educational groups on numerous occasions. I have also written and published many articles about different aspects of Muscle Shoals history. This work is a collection of these historical articles and speeches.

Several changes have been made in these articles since their original presentation and publication. In some cases, articles with similar materials have been combined, and in other cases, parts of articles have been deleted for purposes of clarity. Also, in some cases the titles have been changed to more clearly describe the content. The individual articles do not lend themselves to a chronological arrangement. But the overall collection is generally arranged in a chronological order.

The writer of any historical work will accumulate debts of gratitude to individuals, institutions, and organizations. I am especially grateful for the assistance of the University of North Alabama, the librarians and archivists of the University Library, the staff of the Florence-Lauderdale Public Library, Times Daily, the Tennessee Valley Historical Society and the North Alabama Conference of the United Methodist Church. The assistance given by Richard Sheridan, Terry Pace, Robert Steen and numerous other individuals is especially appreciated.

I am also grateful for the assistance given by my wife Marilyn who critically reviewed most of the articles and made helpful suggestions.

Front Cover: Picture of Muscle Shoals Canal aqueduct over the mouth of Shoals Creek, boat passing through aqueduct, locks on the canal and service railroad by the locks. (Courtesy Richard Sheridan).

Contents

About the Author

Kenneth R. Johnson, a native Alabamian, is Professor emeritus at the University of North Alabama. He grew up in Covington County and graduated from Troy University, The University of Alabama, and Florida State University. Post graduate work was done at the University of Chicago in Black Studies. Professor Johnson taught Southern and Alabama History for over thirty years and published several articles in professional journals. He is a former president of the Tennessee Valley Historical Society and the Alabama Historical Association and a lifetime member of the Southern Historical Association.

Part One: From Indian Mounds to Statehood

Alabama's Tennessee Valley During the Colonial Period

The known history of the people in the Tennessee Valley stretches back about 12,000 years. The first inhabitants were nomadic hunters, following the big game herds and gathering what nature provided. They lived in the Stone Age and had few conveniences other than simple stone tools and the use of fire. Over the next thousands of years while our own early history was being formed in ancient Egypt, the Middle East, Palestine, Greece, and Rome, the early Indians in North Alabama were going through several important changes.

The early Indians gradually learned over thousands of years to improve their technology. The simple stone weapons and tools were gradually replaced with bows and arrows, fish hooks, stone bowls, drills, baskets, and finally pottery. All these and several other discoveries had a profound influence on the early Indians. Pottery more than anything else enhanced the Indians abilities to process, prepare, and preserve food. Thus the Indians gradually took a major step toward maintaining a stable food supply and a better way of life.

A second change that occurred was a slow expansion of this food supply. The Indians were always hunters and gatherers, but this basic source of food gradually began to expand to include fish and other freshwater products especially shell fish. As this change occurred, Indians began to move with the seasons rather than follow the herds of big game. In the spring and summer they gathered food from the land and rivers. In the fall and winter they gathered from the rich nut harvest in the hills and woodlands. Finally about 2500 years ago they learned to farm. Corn, squash, beans, melons and other such plants became standard crops and a part of the Indian diet.

With the development of improved food processing equipment and the growth of agriculture, a third important change came in the Indian life. From their nomadic way of life they gradually began to stay in caves and rock shelters such as Russell Cave near Bridgeport, the Stanley-Worley Shelter in Colbert County, the Trapp Shelter in Franklin County and other places of this nature. But as the rivers became an important source of food, and the Indians began to farm, they tended more and more to leave the caves and rock shelters and settle permanently in villages in the river valleys. Over time the villages grew in size. Houses were log huts with thatched roofs surrounded with log barricades for protection. Fields surrounded the villages outside the barricades. In summary, the

Indians over 10,000 years gradually changed from nomadic hunters and gatherers to a settled life in permanent villages supported by hunting, gathering, fishing, and farming.

As these changes occurred other changes also came about. Gradually, the Indians developed the tribal system with chiefs as leaders. A social system developed in which some members of society were more important than others and a religious system developed with elaborate ceremonies involving temple mounds such as the Indian mound in Florence and others near Decatur and eastern Alabama. When the first Europeans arrived in North America, the Tennessee Valley Indians had many things in common with the people of Europe but there was a vast cultural and technological difference between the two peoples. For example the Indians had no real knowledge of metallurgy. They had no iron weapons or tools. They had no guns or gunpowder, and no printing press or written language. They had not invented the wheel and had no domesticated animals except the dog, which was not used for hunting.

Stanfield-Worley Bluff Shelter (Courtesy Richard Sheridan)

Christopher Columbus showed the way to America in 1492. For the next two hundred years a few explorers passed through the Tennessee Valley, but these left little evidence of their presence except for a few deadly diseases and some domesticated animals. The appearance of the Europeans in North America brought changes very slowly to the Indians of north Alabama.

In the later 17th century this situation began to change. By this time the colonial period was well under way. In 1607 the English established the colony of Virginia. Other colonies followed and by 1700 the English had established South Carolina, North Carolina, Virginia and other colonies to the north of these. Georgia was established a short time later and according to its charter the north Alabama area was part of that colony. All these English colonies claimed the lands west to the Mississippi River and beyond. While the English colonies were developing, the Spanish were firmly entrenched in the Florida area with settlements at St. Augustine and Pensacola. The French were establishing their colonies, also. They claimed the entire Mississippi Valley including the Tennessee Valley and established settlements at Mobile, New Orleans, Natchez, St. Louis and numerous other places in present day Ohio, Indiana, and Illinois. The Tennessee Valley and the major part of the Mississippi Valley were at this early period claimed by the English and the French.

These conflicting territorial claims, made the French and English natural enemies during the colonial period and this struggle over territory was often violent and deadly. But the colonials on both sides were soon engaged in a more serious form of competition. The colonials from both countries wanted the Tennessee Valley for the potentially profitable trade with the Indians. Of course the English also looked to the western areas as land for settlement, for homes and agriculture.

No one knows for sure when the first European hunters and Indian traders came to the Tennessee Valley. We do know that before 1700 trappers and Indian traders out of Charleston, South Carolina, came westward across the Appalachian Mountains and trapped and traded as far west as the Mississippi River. In the year 1700 Jean Couture traveled eastward from the Mississippi River through the Tennessee Valley to Charleston and in the process laid out a route that was often used by other Indian traders in the area. French trappers and traders out of Mobile and Natchez often made their way through the Tennessee Valley in their dealings with the Indians. The rivalry for trade with the Indians was a serious business. Both the English and French colonists wanted the exclusive privilege of trading with the Indians.

The struggle to win control of the Indian trade of the Tennessee Valley continued for almost a century and culminated in the French and Indian War. Both French and English trappers and traders tried to establish close friendly relations with the Indians, mainly the Choctaw, Chickasaw, Creek, and Cherokee. In this competition the English usually won out, primarily because their trade goods were far cheaper than the French. On at least one occasion the French established a temporary trading post in the Shoals area. The English in Charleston drew up plans for a fort to be built at the Muscle Shoals but these plans were never carried through.

Most of the English traders worked out of Charleston and were known in history as the Long Hunters. It was common for them to leave Charleston in the late summer with the pack mules loaded with trade goods. One writer composed a list of items a trader would typically carry with him to trade with the Indians. It included such items as heavy cloth, blankets, axes, broad hoes, salt, brass kettles, hatchets, guns, knives, flints, powder and bullets, tobacco, pipes, rum, petticoats, scissors, thread, needles, red girdles, linen shirts, coats, hats, looking glasses and other such items. These Long Hunters often ranged westward to the Mississippi River and returned to Charleston two years later with their pack mules loaded with skins. This was big business. From 1700 to 1763 and average of 50,000 deer skins were shipped out from Charleston each year. Also, a large number of beaver and buffalo skins were shipped.

The extensive trade carried on by the French and English with the Indians had a major impact in the Tennessee Valley. The great herds of wild animals declined rapidly. The life style of the Indians changed. Indians wanted the goods offered by the traders, and their main item of commerce was the pelts. Hence the Indians gradually became commercial hunters rather than hunting for food. Also, the Indians gradually became dependent on the manufactured goods sold by the French and English. By the time of the American Revolution, the Indians had given up many of their old production methods and depended upon trade for their weapons, tools and other necessities.

The struggle for the control of the Tennessee Valley and other parts of the frontier began about 1700 and continued with varying degrees of intensity until it culminated in the French and Indian War. This war ended with the Treaty of Paris in 1763, twelve years before the American Revolution. By the terms of the treaty, the French gave up their claim to all land in North America, and England gained title to the North Alabama area.

By the end of the French and Indian War in 1763, the Tennessee River valley was a familiar place to Indian traders, but was little known to the rest of the world. No attempt had been made to study and map the area. This situation soon changed. In 1769, just six years before the outbreak of the American Revolution, a Lt. Thomas Hutchins, an engineer with the British Army, make the first scientific study of the Tennessee River and the adjacent areas. Actually Lt. Hutchins was ordered to carry out a two-fold mission. He was ordered to patrol the western rivers and intercept French and Spanish traders who were trading illegally in English territory. He was also ordered to keep a journal describing the topographical features and navigational problems encountered along the rivers. To carry out his orders, Lt. Hutchins purchased a boat from a trading firm in Kaskaskia. The boat was named the "Gage" in honor of General Thomas Gage, the commanding general in the English colonies at that time. The boat was propelled with twenty-four oars and carried one large brass six-pound cannon. It carried a crew of thirty-five men with supplies sufficient for six months. Lt. Hutchins apparently carried out the assignment rather well. Starting at the mouth of the Tennessee, he navigated 900 miles upriver. He observed and described the serious problems to navigation created by the Muscle Shoals and also the Suck in east Alabama. With crude instruments, he took compass readings, measured distances, and made rough sketches for later use in mapmaking. His reports were not totally correct but considering the difficulties involved in his work, it was surprisingly accurate. Lt. Hutchins' map of the Tennessee River area did not appear in print until after the American Revolution, but it certainly was instrumental in educating people about the Tennessee River and the area of North Alabama.

There was no obvious connection between the Tennessee Valley and the American Revolution which began in 1775. The Tennessee Valley had no influence on the course of the Revolution. But the Revolution had an influence on the Tennessee Valley area. About sixteen months after the Revolution started, the Second Continental Congress adopted the Declaration of Independence. At that time, there were no settlements in the North Alabama area. Not one settler had built a log cabin or cleared farm land in the valley. Actually, Alabama's Tennessee Valley was far to the west of the settled areas of North Carolina, South Carolina, and Georgia. The westward movement of these settlers were blocked by the powerful Cherokee nation. But the American Revolution changed this. About six months after the Declaration of Independence was adopted, war broke out between the Cherokee Indians, who supported the English, and the frontier militia, who favored American independence. After several months of fighting the Cherokees were defeated in two major battles and forced to make large land concessions. While the Cherokee nation was not destroyed as a nation or as a military force, their power to block western expansion was broken. It was only a matter of time until the land hungry frontiersmen pushed westward into Tennessee and North Alabama.

Indian Trails

Long before Europeans arrived on this continent, early Indians developed and followed trails through the thick forest of the Tennessee River Valley. Over time some of these trails have evolved into modern highways, but most have returned to their original wilderness condition.

Prehistoric Indians had little need for anything more than paths or trails through the forest. Indians did not use metal tools therefore did not have the means of smoothing the surface or clearing roadways. Also, they did not use the wheel, hence load-carrying vehicles were not in use. Very little commerce was carried on between the tribes. The trails gradually developed out of use rather than any form of planned construction. These trails were very narrow, little improved and poorly marked.

The Indians usually traveled in single file and sometimes they got lost while trying to follow their own trails. When whites started using these trails, they had an even more difficult time. In the early 1800's, Lorenzo Dow, a prominent Methodist preacher, lost his way while following an Indian trail through South Alabama. Several hours were spent wandering lost in the forest before he found the trail and continued his journey.

No set criteria existed for selecting the site of Indian trails. As in all their ways of life, the Indians simply used what nature offered. The trails usually followed the high grounds thereby avoiding swamps, rivers, steep hills and mountains, etc. The high grounds offered solid footing and an element of protection against surprise attacks. Crossing rivers was difficult. Fords and "footlogs" over streams were very helpful and much appreciated by travelers.

The trails served the Indians much like the modern highway system serves people today. Apparently most trails through the Tennessee Valley forest simply connected villages. It is very likely that over hundreds of years, several trails existed in the Shoals area north and south of the Tennessee River. Many trails changed with the seasons and with the relocation of villages. Other trails, connected villages with hunting grounds. Some covered great distances. Records indicate that it was not unusual for hunters to travel from Alabama and Mississippi to Kentucky blue grass country on hunting trips.

The "Chickasaw Trail", which began in central Mississippi was used mainly by hunters. It extended from Mississippi through the Muscle Shoals area into Kentucky.

Another trail with a more confusing purpose, was the "High Town Path." It was located along the high ground that separated the streams that flowed northward into the Tennessee River and the streams that flowed southward into the Gulf. Boundaries between Indian tribes were not clearly marked. Some historians claim that the main purpose of the High Town Path was to serve as boundary between the Creek and Cherokee Indians. It is also possible that this trail extended to Savannah, Georgia where Indians carried on trade with the English colonists.

The prehistoric period of regional history ended about 1540 when Spanish explorer, Hernando de Soto, explored the southeastern part of the United States. Over the next 250 years the Spanish, French, and English traders made good use of trails while exploring the country, hunting, and carrying on trade with the Indians. These early traders with their pack animals traveled and used the trails much like the Indians. They did not need or try to build wagon roads, or make significant improvements on the Indian trails. But the rivers were also important in the conduct of trade through the Indian country.

In the 1700's French and English traders began coming to the Muscle Shoals area. The French came northward from early Mobile and others came southward from settlements north of the Ohio River. They established no permanent forts or trading post in the area. Most traders lived and traded with the Indians for a few weeks and then moved on. English traders, called the "Long Hunters," came into the Shoals area from Charleston, South Carolina and Savannah, Georgia.

Over the years in the 17th and 18th centuries, the Indians of Alabama and Mississippi became increasingly familiar with European manufactured goods. They also, became more dependent on these goods. This growing dependency brought further changes in the Indian way of life. Indians became commercial hunters rather than subsistence hunters. Also, instead of waiting for traders to come to their villages, Indians increasingly carried their skins and other products to trading centers such as Fort Toulouse, Fort Loudoun, Pensacola, and Mobile where they could get better prices and choose from a bigger selection of trade goods. With this new method of trading, new trails gradually emerged connecting these trading centers with villages in the hinterland. Thus the traditional Indian trails were often changed over time. Many old trails faded and new trails came into being.

During colonial times dishonest traders often cheated the Indians and thereby created trouble between Native Americans and whites settlers. While George Washington was president in the 1790's, the United States government established trading posts for carrying on trade with the Indians. These government trading posts represented an attempt to carry on helpful, honest, and convenient trade between the white people and the Indians.

Indians brought otter, beaver, raccoon, fox, "cat," bear, wolf and deer skins to the trading posts to exchange for manufactured goods. In addition to skins the Indians traded beeswax, snakeroot, tallow, bear oil, corn, beans, beef, bacon, venison, and other such products to the earlier white traders and settlers. In exchange for these products the Indians obtained blankets, strouds, calico, silver jewelry, knives, gunpowder, lead, vermilion, kettles, wool hats, salt, sugar, coffee, cowbells, saddles, tools, and other such manufactured articles.

This trade usually took the form of barter. Very little paper money or gold and silver coin was in circulation on the frontier and the Indians had no gold or silver mines. They simply traded what they could harvest from nature.

The government trading posts were also used by the early white settlers. These settlers were farmers rather than hunters. But like the Indians they exchanged their produce for the trade goods.

By the late 1700's the old Indian trails were losing their significance. Only roads could meet the needs of settled communities, the U.S. military, the growing commerce and many varieties of government service. As the Indians increasingly adopted the white man's way of life they found that trails or paths through the forest were not adequate to meet their needs.

While most of the Indian trails were gradually reclaimed by nature, a few were converted into roads. The Chickasaw Trace, better known as the Natchez Trace, is a good example.

From Indian Trails to Roads

In the first decade of the 19th century, the national government faced the need for roads in the Southwestern part of the United States as it then existed. Most of the area which is now known as Mississippi and Alabama was then known as the Mississippi Territory. Natchez was the capital of the Territory. Washington County, the first county in Alabama, was made up of several settlements. It included such places as Fort Stoddart, St. Stephens, and other communities along the lower Tombigbee River. Not a single road connected any of these settlements to the nearest settled areas in Tennessee and Georgia.

The first roads though the Muscle Shoals area represented an attempt by the United States government to connect early settlements to the established towns already existing in Tennessee.

In 1801, with the approval of the Choctaw and Chickasaw Indians, the US government converted the Chickasaw Trace into what became known as the Natchez Trace. The winding barely recognizable trail was widened and improved by the US Army in 1801. But it still remained a trail only wide enough for man and animals to walk in single file. Nevertheless, it was the first land route connecting the Natchez area with Nashville.

George Colbert Home (Courtesy Richard Sheridan)

But the early Trace was obviously inadequate. It was a footpath not a wagon road and there were no facilities to accommodate the travelers with food and lodging. The only improvements on the Trace at that early time in the Muscle Shoals area was George Colbert's Ferry which was located about sixteen miles below the Shoals.

By 1810, the US government had with Indian approval converted the Natchez Trace into a roadway with numerous "Stands" along the way offering food and lodging to travelers. George Colbert who operated his ferry from 1801 to 1819 not only transported people and their property across the Tennessee River, he provided food, lodging, blacksmith, and other services for travelers. About eight miles south of George Colbert's Ferry, Levi Colbert operated a stand on the banks of Buzzard Roost Creek where he offered "entertainment" for travelers. Still further southward on the Trace, James Colbert operated a stand for the benefit of travelers.

Most of the traffic on the Natchez Trace before 1821 was moving northward. Generally when people living in Tennessee and Kentucky wanted to take their products to the New Orleans market, they simply traveled down river on flatboats or rafts. In those days before the steamboat, they traveled back northward over the Trace. Travel over the Trace was filled with danger and adventure which has been well described by Jonathan Daniels in his book The Devil's Backbone.

Although the Natchez Trace has long been considered a part of Muscle Shoals history, it did not contribute greatly to the development of the region. The Trace bypassed the heart of the Shoals. Also, with the coming of the steamboat in 1821 and the building of other roads, the Natchez Trace started a rapid decline in the 1820's.

Even before the Trace started declining as a major thoroughfare, it had lost most of its earlier connection with the Indians and their use of the trail.

Land Speculators Attempt the First Settlement of the Muscle Shoals Area

The oldest and youngest county in Alabama had the same name, Houston. The youngest Alabama county, created in 1903, is located in the Southeast corner of the State with Dothan as its county seat.

The first county, in what later became north Alabama was named Houston. At the time, 1783, the American Revolution was coming to an end. The whole region was a part of the State of Georgia. No white settlers lived in the area.

A group of prominent North Carolina and Virginia businessmen formed a private company for the purpose of establishing a colony in the Muscle Shoals area.

They hoped that this colony would be like the settlements Daniel Boone and Richard Henderson were establishing in Kentucky. They hoped to get large land grants and sell the land to westward-moving immigrants.

These developers began their operations by purchasing the Cherokee Indians' claim to the land in the Shoals area. Actually, the Cherokee occupied very little of the land. The claims of the Chickasaw and Creek Indians to the Muscle Shoals area were simply ignored, although the Chickasaw actually occupied the land.

The developers thought the Muscle Shoals area was in North Carolina. But finding that it was part of Georgia, they started lobbying the Georgia legislature for large land grants and for the creation of a county government. At this point several prominent Georgians were brought into the venture. The Georgia legislature was cooperative and authorized the creation of Houston County which embraced all the territory currently lying between the Tennessee River and the southern boundary of Tennessee.

Seven commissioners were appointed by the Georgia legislature to survey the region and establish a county government. Probably the best known of these commissioners were John Sevier, John Donelson, William Blunt, and Joseph Martin.

In July 1784, the Commissioners met in the Muscle Shoals area to plan and establish a county government. Sevier was named commander of the militia. John Donelson became the county surveyor, and Joseph Martin was appointed Indian agent.

None of the commissioners and no settlers lived in or near the new county. To officially open the county and entice settlers to the Muscle Shoals area, a great land sale was planned for March 1785. It was to be held at the Martin Trading Post on the Holston

River in what is today eastern Tennessee. This first effort by Americans to develop the Muscle Shoals area seemed to be off to a good start.

But appearances were deceiving. The land was never surveyed and the great land sale was never held. Several conditions led to a declining interest in the project.

The Chickasaw Indian influence was great. Several chiefs requested that there be no white encroachment on their hunting lands. They also talked of forming an alliance with the Creek Indians against the white settlers.

Equally important was the fact that none of the developers had plans to move to or live in the Muscle Shoals area. Also, Sevier, Donelson, and others became deeply involved in other business matters and in the political activities of the States of Franklin and Tennessee.

The first organized effort to settle and develop the Muscle Shoals area failed completely. But it did call attention to the great potential of the area, and many other ambitious men were eager to develop their own project.

Gaines Trace – A Forgotten Thoroughfare

On the cold winter morning of December 26, 1807, twelve years before Alabama became a state in the union, Captain Edmund P. Gaines of the United States Army set out on an important mission. Orders from Secretary of War Henry Dearborn directed him to survey out a road from Melton's Bluff on the south side of the Tennessee River across what are today Morgan, Lawrence, and Franklin counties to Cotton Gin Port on the headwaters of the Tombigbee River in Mississippi. Gaines and his small crew spent the next eighteen days surveying an 89-mile long route through some of the toughest country in Alabama. During the entire period, the surveying party crossed no roads and saw no settlers or other evidence of white man's civilization.

Captain Gaines was experienced in this kind of work. Some people thought he was the best surveyor in the U. S. Army. At an earlier time he had helped survey parts of the Natchez Trace. In 1802 he had laid out a road which was never developed from the head of navigation on Bear Creek in the head waters of the Black Warrior River.

Gaines and his party were lucky. Most of the leaves had shed from the trees enhancing visibility. Also, much to their relief they saw no Chickasaw Indians, who owned the territory through which they were passing, until the day before the project was complete. Even these Indians were friendly. The weather on the other hand was miserably cold and rainy with some snow and ice. To add to their discomfort they began to run out of food during the last few days.

Ice Clogged the Muscle Shoals in 1918

A few of the larger streams such as Town Creek and Bear Creek had been given names by early explorers but most of the creeks and branches were unnamed.

Gaines made an elaborate set of notes in which he described the beauty of the terrain, the trees, and many of the problems he encountered. These notes are housed in the Tennessee State Archives. A major problem was finding fording places on the numerous streams. He sought places where the river banks were low, the water was shallow, and the river bottoms covered with small rocks. The surveyors sometimes spent whole days traveling up and down streams searching for a good fording place.

The surveying party had no authority or equipment to actually build a road. But they did mark out the road with "two chops and a blaze" on the "front and rear" of all trees along the route.

Shortly after the road was laid out, George S. Gaines, the surveyor's younger brother, was appointed by the Secretary of War to negotiate a treaty with the Chickasaw for the right to build a wagon road along the route. The unpredictable nature of the Indians quickly became evident. At first the Chickasaw leaders were eager for the road and several of them mentioned places along the route where they wanted to build stands to provide food, drink, and quarters for travelers along the road. But their early enthusiasm gradually turned to opposition. They refused to permit the construction of a wagon road. But in 1810 they did approve the clearing of a "horsepath" along the surveyed route. When this path was opened, it became known as "Gaines Trace" in honor of these two brothers.

The building of a road through the forest connecting two rather insignificant villages, Melton's Bluff and Cotton Gin Port, both of which later completely disappeared, seems to have been a great waste. Such did not appear to be the case at that time. Two arguments were advanced to justify the building of the road. First, many early settlers came down the Tennessee River with plans to go to St. Stephens, Fort Stoddart, Coffeeville, and other settlements along the lower Tombigbee River. At that time there was no route for settlers to travel south from the Tennessee Valley to these settlements in southwest Alabama about fifty miles north of Mobile. Gaines Trace would permit travelers to come down the Tennessee River to Melton's Bluff at which point they could proceed over Gaines Trace to Cotton Gin Port where they could travel down the Tombigbee River on a raft, flatboat, or pirogue. Also , in the early 1800's the merchants living in the Tombigbee settlements needed to import many products for their customers and supplies for the army at Fort Stoddart. At that time the Spanish owned West Florida which gave them control of the entire gulf coastline including Mobile and Mobile River through which all exported and imported goods must pass. The Spanish used their control of this trade route to impose numerous restrictions and high import-export duties on goods passing through their territory. This caused the American settlers real hardship and very high cost. For example, a barrel of flour sold in Natchez for $4. The same barrel of flour in St. Stephens brought in through Mobile would cost $16.

It was widely believed that the Gaines Trace would provide a cheaper means of bringing needed goods and supplies into the Tombigbee settlement. It was expected that products, like people, would move down the Tennessee River to Melton's Bluff and then over land to Cotton Gin Port and from there down the Tombigbee River to the frontier settlements. The Gaines Trace was expected to be a vital link in this transportation plan.

While the Gaines Trace did provide some improved means of transportation through the unsettled land, it never measured up to expectations. It certainly did not become a popular thoroughfare like the Natchez Trace.

Later historical developments reduced the importance of the Gaines Trace. In 1813 the United States seized control of the Mobile area from the Spanish and opened up travel along the Mobile and Tombigbee Rivers to the settlements there. At about the same time the steamboat came into common use in the southern part of Alabama. Hence the original purpose of the Trace lost most of its significance.

With the passage of time the city of Decatur grew and completely overshadowed Melton's Bluff. Cotton Gin Port also lost its significance and gradually disappeared.

Shortly after the Indians gave up their title to most of the land in Alabama in 1817, settlers began pouring into northwest Alabama. By 1818 Morgan, Lawrence, and Franklin counties were created. Gaines Trace became a wagon road, serving local needs, not connecting two rivers systems. Several settlements such as Courtland, Russellville, Belgreen, and others were founded along the Trace. Russellville founded by land speculators in 1820, was situated at the intersection of Gaines Trace and the Jackson Military Road.

The name "Gaines Trace" gradually passed out of common use but the roadway remain in service. In general the modern state highway number 24 follows the roadway laid out by Captain Gaines many years ago.

Muscle Shoals Important To South Alabama Settlements

While the Natchez Trace opened a land route between Nashville and Natchez, it offered very little help to persons traveling or transporting goods south to the settlements like Fort Stoddart, St. Stephens, and other settlements along the lower Tombigbee River.

In the year 1800 the United States Government built a cotton gin at the headwaters of the Tombigbee River in the edge of Mississippi. The community that quickly grew up about the gin and at this shipping point became known as Cotton Gin Port. This town thrived for several years, but according to legend the Chickasaw Indians burned the gin and the community gradually disappeared.

No trails or roads connected the Tennessee River with the Tombigbee River. But it was common for travelers to come down the Tennessee to the head of the Muscle Shoals. There they would leave the river and travel through the uncleared forest to Cotton Gin Port where they would travel down the Tombigbee to the settlements that made up Washington County, the first county in Alabama. The absence of any roads or trails through the forest made this practice very difficult and dangerous. Also, it was impossible to transport wagons or commercial goods between the two rivers.

In July 1807 the Secretary of War ordered Lt. Edmund Pendleton Gaines to survey and mark out a road from the head of the Muscle Shoals to Cotton Gin Port and a road from the foot of the Shoals to Cotton Gin Port. In late January 1808 Gaines reported the task complete. A road, eighty nine miles long was marked out between the head of the Muscle Shoals (near Decatur) and Cotton Gin Port. This road was soon cleared and made into what was known as the Gaines Trace. The road marked out from the foot of the Muscles Shoals to Cotton Gin Port was never constructed probably because the Chickasaw Indians objected and because there were very few travelers and settlers in the Shoals area at that time.

Several people suggested that the Natchez Trace should be rerouted so that it would pass through Cotton Gin Port. As early as 1802, Lt. Gaines had marked out a road between Cotton gin Port and Colbert's Ferry on orders from General James Wilkinson. But the Chickasaw strongly objected and the road was never opened. They did however agree to the opening of a trail for use by individual travelers and pack mules. A trail of this type would serve no good purpose, hence it was never opened.

In 1808 Lt. Gaines recommended to the Secretary of War that the Natchez Trace be rerouted so that travelers coming northward would come to Cotton Gin Port and from there they would travel over the Gaines Trace to the Decatur area and then on to Nashville. He argued that the distance from Natchez to Nashville would be shorter and the road would be better and drier. Opening of this route would have taken business away from the Colbert brothers, especially George Colbert and his ferry. The Colberts sent strongly worded objections to President Thomas Jefferson claiming the Chickasaw Indians as a people would be seriously hurt. The route of the Natchez Trace was never changed.

Most people seemed to have difficulty doing business with the Colberts unless the Colberts made money. Lt. Gaines angrily denounced George Colbert on several occasions claiming that he always identified Chickasaw interest with what was good for him personally.

In this early decade, little thought was given to building roads within the Muscle Shoals because no towns or counties existed in the areas until 1818 and very few settlers resided in the area. In fact the US government was far more interested in moving squatters off Indian lands than building roads to serve them.

White Man's Removal

Most Alabamian have heard of the Indian Removal and some feel a deep sympathy for the Indians when the "Trail of Tears" is discussed. The story of the White Man's Removal should also be told.

In 1806 the United States government purchased the Cherokee Indian's claim to all the land north of the Tennessee River and west of the "Old Chickasaw Fields" except one large track of land that became known as Chief Doublehead's Reserve. Soon after the Cherokee claims were extinguished, white settlers began moving southward out of Tennessee into the area we now know as Lauderdale and Limestone counties. These "squatters" confidently expected to settle on good land, improve it, and when the land was surveyed and put up for sale, they could buy it for $2.00 per acre.

Their hopes were somewhat dimmed when James Robertson, who was surveying the boundary lines, spread the word in 1807 that the Chickasaw Indians also claimed this land and they had not yet sold their claim to the U.S. government. This Chickasaw claim might have worried the settlers but did not deter their moving into the area. By 1808 well over 200 families lived in the area. Some squatted on public land while others were legitimately leasing land in the Doublehead Reserve. But most settlers simply squatted on the Chickasaw lands.

In December 1808 during the closing months of President Thomas Jefferson's administration, the Secretary of War ordered the U. S. Army to remove all settlers from the Indian lands. In a fifty-one day sweep through the area by troops commanded by Colonel Return J. Meigs, Cherokee Indian Agent, at Hiwassee Garrison in east Tennessee, 201 families were removed from Chickasaw lands and 83 families from Cherokee lands.

The removal was carried out without resistance or problems except for one sick person and some women late in pregnancy.

A few of the settlers moved over into Madison County but most moved back northward into Tennessee. Meigs pointed out in his report that "forbearance and humanity" had been exercised and that in compliance with President Jefferson's policies, the cabins, fences and crops of the settlers had not been destroyed.

No arrangements were made to help the settlers or for keeping them off the Chickasaw lands once they were removed. The hardships they experienced and the continued existence of their cabins and crops was almost an open invitation to return. And they did return in increasing numbers.

By mid-1810 at least 450 and probably over 2000 settlers lived in what would become Lauderdale and Limestone counties. In June of that year the Secretary of War in the James Madison administration, ordered another removal. On this occasion notice was given to the settlers, and a reasonable time allowed to remove their "effects" and crops. But after this removal, all cabins and fences were to be burned. Also following this removal, soldiers were ordered to patrol the area to see that squatters did not return.

To carry out this directive a continuing military presence was needed in the Muscle Shoals area. To meet this need the Secretary of War ordered the building of a "post or station" consisting of log houses adequate to house two companies of soldiers, officers, and such animals and such supplies as might be needed. This "encampment," located in the east Lauderdale County area, soon became known as "Fort Hampton" in honor of General Wade Hampton, a Revolutionary War veteran. This fort was intended to be temporary with no major fortifications because no military threats existed in the area.

Apparently Fort Hampton existed for about four years from late 1810 to 1814. It was located a short distance east of Elk River and about one-fourth mile north of highway 72.

Apparently during these four years some families were removed. But the number of settlers in the Lauderdale and Limestone area certainly increased considerably. Their presence probably helped persuade the Chickasaw Indians to give up their claim to the land in 1816. Regardless of Chickasaw actions, the settlers felt they had a right to settle on the land. They fought vigorously to enjoy that right.

When the U.S. Army was trying to remove white settlers from land claimed by the Chickasaw Indians, the settlers felt that they were being treated unjustly. They made every effort possible to remain on the land.

In early 1809 when Colonel Return J. Meigs came to remove the intruders, they sought and were granted a short delay in order to get Chickasaw permission to remain on the land. A delegation visited a very unsympathetic Chief George Colbert at his ferry on the Tennessee River. Colbert claimed that the settlers knew they were on Indian lands and should remove themselves from the land immediately. Their request to stay until their crops were harvested aroused even less sympathy. The removal was carried out and 284 families were removed.

The following year when the second removal was being considered about 450 settlers around the "Sims' Settlement" near the Elk River drew up and submitted to the President and Congress a petition arguing that they should be permitted to remain on the land.

First the petition emphasized their innocence of wrong doing. It stated that many settlers came to the land as early as the spring of 1807 without any knowledge or intention of violating the laws of the government or infringing on the right of another nation. The settlers believed or claimed to believe that the land had been purchased by the government, hence it was public land, and they had the right to settle on it.

The petitioners denigrated the Chickasaw claim to the land. It was pointed out that at an earlier time the Chickasaw Indians had not claimed the land. They also argued that the Chickasaw did not need the land. It was estimated that every man in the Chickasaw nation had 100,000 acres of land which they roamed over like many wolves or bears. The settlers stated that "Indian lands" were of no use to the government or society and should be open to white settlement.

The settlers argued that their use of the land would be of great value to the government and the country. They felt it unjust that settlers were forced to rent poor stony ridges to rear their families while there were fine fertile lands lying uncultivated.

This unfriendly attitude toward the Indians was common at that time. One writer stated that "tribes of savages" throughout the country contrive to keep our mails and citizens exposed to all the dangers and inconveniencies of an extensive wilderness.

The petitioners never doubted but that the Chickasaw would someday give up their claim to the land. The settlers begged the leaders in Washington to let them stay on the land "as tenants at will" until the Chickasaw decided to sell their claims to the land.

The petitioners also sought to establish their own good character. It was stated that they were not a set of dishonest people who were fleeing from the laws of their state. Colonel Meigs in his report tried to confirm this assessment. He wrote that although the settlers were aggressors, many of them were reputable, well-informed, and rich in cattle and horses. He further stated that the settlers were generally not a criminal element seeking to evade their public duty, civil or military.

The petitioners also sought mercy. They pointed out that in settling this country many respectable men had died leaving widows with families and orphan children. The petitioners pleaded with government leaders to think what was to become of these poor orphan families who needed friendly help instead of orders executed on them by an "unfeeling world." They argued that the government leaders should not bring women and children to a state of starvation merely to gratify a heathen nation.

Finally the petitioners stated that according to their best calculations 2250 souls lived on Chickasaw land and all could live "tolerably" well if permitted to remain on their improved lands. But if removed, the families would be brought to a deplorable condition because they could not take much of their property with them and could not afford to purchase more.

There is no clear evidence that the settlers' arguments had any influence in Washington, but their movement into the Lauderdale and Limestone county area laid the foundation for future growth.

The Jackson Military Road

In late 1814 Andrew Jackson was trying to move a large army from Mobile through the swamps and thick forest of southern Mississippi and Louisiana to New Orleans. In most places no roads or settlements existed. Pathways had to be cleared for wagons and artillery pieces.

Of course Jackson's Army did arrive in time to thoroughly defeat the invading British army in the Battle of New Orleans in 1815, the last and most famous battle in the War of 1812.

Jackson then had the problem of moving approximately 7500 soldiers back to their homes in Tennessee. They traveled over the "river road" to Natchez and then up the Natchez Trace. At nearly all points the roads and bridges were poorly maintained; traveling was slow and difficult.

After these experiences Major General Andrew Jackson recommended to Secretary of War William Crawford that a federal road be constructed from Columbia, Tennessee to Madisonville, Louisiana.

It was thought that such a road would offer several advantages. An army could be moved swiftly to the Gulf Coast if another enemy invasion should occur. Also, this proposed road would shorten the traveling distance between Nashville and New Orleans by about 250 miles. This would be helpful to the postal service, businessmen, and ordinary travelers.

Jackson's recommendation made its way to Congress and in September 1816, $5000 was appropriated to begin the project. General Jackson was placed in charge; all work on the project was by the US military forces.

The route was laid out southwestwardly from Columbia, Tennessee. Major William O. Butler laid out the first ninety miles and Captain Hugh Young surveyed the route through Alabama, Mississippi, and Louisiana to Madisonville. After crossing the Tennessee state line, the surveyors passed through no towns or large settlements. But while construction was in progress, Florence, Tuscumbia, Russellville, Sulligent, and other places in Alabama, and Columbus, Mississippi were founded on or near the Jackson Military Road.

Construction began in May 1817. An average of 300 men worked on the road including sawyers, carpenters, blacksmiths, and ordinary laborers. They were furnished oxen, traveling forges, and numerous kinds of construction equipment.

The military road was planned to be 40 feet wide throughout, but in some cases it was reduced to 25 feet. No attempt was made to build a solid foundation. Trees were cut as near the ground as practicable leaving the stump with a concave top in order to accelerate decay. Trees were cut in convenient lengths and rolled to the side of the cleared roadway.

Most of the construction difficulties occurred southwest of the Tombigbee River. In the low swampy area south of Columbus 35 "neat and substantial bridges" from 60 to 200 feet long were built and 20,000 feet of causeways was laid. The causeways were laid over marshy spots by placing small timbers close together in a latitudinal direction to the road. Dirt was strewn over the timbers thereby elevating these parts of the road to a higher level and giving it a harder surface. This type of construction is sometimes called a corduroy road.

Jackson Military Road (Courtesy Robert Steen)

Ferries were placed in operation over the larger rivers. For example the ferry over the Tennessee River at Florence was operating well before the town was established in 1818.

Road construction, like the surveying, started at the northern most point and moved southward. The entire area was almost totally unpopulated. Below Columbus, Mississippi the road passed mainly through the Chickasaw and Choctaw nations. This presented no problem.

The Jackson Military Road was officially completed in May 1820, after approximately 75,801 days of labor were expended over three years by soldiers in the First and Eighth Infantry Regiments.

To pay for the project Congress appropriated at least $20,000. Recent historians claim the road cost about $300,000. They arrive at this figure by estimating the cost of soldier's pay, clothing, food, and maintenance along with the cost of animals and equipment.

When the Military Road was completed, General Jackson estimated that the government could now send mail from Nashville to New Orleans by stagecoach in seventeen days and travelers would find this route 208 miles shorter than the Natchez Trace. He confidently predicted that the Jackson Military Road would become the most important road in America.

There are no great adventure stories making up the history of the Jackson Military Road. In this respect the road is completely overshadowed by the Natchez Trace.

The Military Road through south Tennessee and northwest Alabama mainly served local travelers among the settled communities. Also, travelers were generally not carrying large sums of money like many of the travelers on the Natchez Trace. Also, there were organized law enforcement authorities in most of Tennessee and Alabama. This certainly deterred crime along this part of the roadway.

One story did survive. Two brothers from Kentucky drove a string of twenty-seven horses south on the Military Road in 1819 and 1820. Their biggest adventure was their contact with the Chickasaw and Choctaw Indians.

The road had no stands or inns to serve travelers. When night found them in the Chickasaw Nation, they arranged to spend the night in the home of an Indian family. The house was "a wigwam with puncheon floor." The building had no chimney or fireplace. A fire burned in the center of the one room and smoke escaped through a hole in the roof.

The Indian family members were not hostile but neither were they friendly. They made no effort to communicate with travelers beyond what was absolutely necessary.

Five barefooted children between ages of about four and twelve "with britch clothes passing between their legs" slept in the loft of the wigwam. They had learned a little English: "Gimme hogmeat" was their main contribution to conversation.

The entire group including the two travelers, the "old man and his squaw" and the five children slept in one room with deer and bear skins as their beds and their covers.

The horses were penned in a lot with a good trough and were fed corn and fodder. The younger traveler had some fear of the Indians. He watched them carefully. Early the next morning, the brothers paid their bill, harnessed their horses, and left.

They were soon in the Choctaw Nation. There they had good food and a warm welcome from one of the "great Indian Chiefs." The Chief owned several slaves and operated a good farm. He was dressed in moccasins, long leggings, and a long ruffled shirt. He wore a large strand of beads on this neck with his hair tied in a large pigtail on top of this head, wrapped with a red ribbon.

After selling the chief a horse, the horse-driving travelers left the Military Road and traveled to Mobile before going on to New Orleans where there was a ready market for the horses.

The Military Road had a significant influence in northwest Alabama even through it never became the national highway its supporters envisioned.

The road helped determine the location of some towns. Russellville was founded at the intersection of the Gaines Trace and the Military Road. Further southward Columbus, Mississippi was established about two years after the road was constructed at the point where the road crossed the Tombigbee River.

The Big Spring in Franklin (later Colbert) County more than anything else determined the location of Tuscumbia. But the Road was the main north-south highway in the area and it passed by the east side of the springs.

The founders of Florence deliberately located the town at the foot of the Muscle Shoals. But the existence of the Military Road and the ferry that crossed the Tennessee near this site made it all the more desirable.

In the 1820's the Military Road was the primary road between the Muscle Shoals and Nashville. As such it was certainly one of the main paths followed by settlers moving into the area.

Actually the laying out of towns helped bring on the end of part of the road. When Tuscumbia was surveyed it was laid out in a rectangular pattern with streets and avenues running in straight lines which did not fit the curves in the already existing Military Road. Over time the road lost its identity as the streets were cleared and opened for public transportation.

In Florence the same thing happened. As the streets/avenues west of Court Street were opened, the Road ceased to exist. East of Court Street, the town extended northward to the Military Road but did not interrupt it. Later as the town grew, the road became known as Hermitage Drive. It was altered to fit the needs of the growing town. But some of the old road still exists and is known as the "Military Road."

Many of the towns through which the Jackson Military Road passed still have the streets or highways named for the road.

Jackson Military Road was a Great Disappointment

The Jackson Military Road was a great disappointment. It never became a great frontier highway that Andrew Jackson and others envisioned. Within ten years after the road was completed in May 1820 most of it in Mississippi was unusable.

There were several reason for the failure of the Jackson Military Road. The military never needed the road. There was no invasion of the U.S. along the Gulf Coast by a foreign power. Hence the U. S. military, including General Andrew Jackson, lost interest in the project.

Also, steamboats began to travel western rivers. The first steamboat came up the Tennessee River from New Orleans arriving in Florence in 1820, the year the Jackson Military Road was officially opened. Steamboats changed travel routes. Steamboat travel was faster, cheaper, safer, and more enjoyable than traveling over frontier roads.

Persons traveling between Nashville and New Orleans found river boats preferable to roadways. With few exceptions people did not travel over the Military Road except in Alabama and Tennessee where settlers used it for mainly local needs. Even the Natchez Trace declined in importance as travelers started using the steamboat.

Travelers going southward on the Jackson Military Road faced another problem when they arrived at the Madisonville, Louisiana, the southern terminus. They were still about 60 miles from New Orleans. This final leg of a journey to New Orleans required a boat ride across Lake Pontchartrain. At least one passenger while crossing the lake became seasick and complained "I have never been so sick in my life."

Within ten years after the completion of the Military Road, most of the roadway had fallen into disuse. The 150 miles below Columbus, Mississippi was reported to be impassable for wheel carriages. Bushes quickly grew up in the roadway and many trees had blown over blocking the road. Most causeways and bridges were dangerous and unusable. Many had been completely destroyed by floods and other such acts of nature.

The United State Postal Service never used the Jackson Military Road for transporting the mail. In 1825 the Postmaster General reported that the road was so much out of repair, as to render the regular transportation of the mail upon it impracticable.

In one respect the Jackson Military Road was doomed to failure from the beginning. No provision was made by the national or state governments to maintain the road. Hence no maintenance was performed except in Tennessee and Alabama where communities repaired the road to satisfy their local needs.

Much of the Military Road in Alabama and Tennessee continued in general use, but it served mainly local needs. It did not function as a national highway.

Andrew Jackson must have lost some faith in the importance of the Military Road. When he became president of the United States in 1829, he made no attempt to upgrade and maintain this federal road.

South Port, the Earliest White Settlement in the Muscle Shoals

South Port, located on the south side of the Tennessee River at the foot of the Muscle Shoals, was probably the first white settlement in the Shoals area.

It was founded in 1813, before any of the counties or cities in northwest Alabama came into existence. Five years later in 1818, it became a part of Franklin County when it was established by the Territorial Legislature.

There is some argument as to the exact location of South Port. One writer claims that this "business center" grew up at the south landing of the Tennessee River ferry on the old trail that became the Military Road in 1817. Actually, the location was about a mile up river between present day O'Neal and Singing River Bridges, almost directly across the river from downtown Florence.

Today all evidence of the early settlement has disappeared except for deep cuts in the embankments where wagons made their way down to the water's edge. A historical marker, situated beside the TVA Walking Trail, gives some indication of the location of South Port.

Many of the towns in the Shoals area were founded by land speculators. But South Port came into existence mainly to meet the real needs of very early settlers on the south side of the Tennessee River in what is today Morgan, Lawrence, Franklin, and Colbert Counties. These early settlers grew cotton and a few other commercial products. To sell these products, they were brought by wagon to South Port where they were loaded onto rafts or flat boats for floating down river to markets in New Orleans.

South Port was ideally situated to meet the docking, loading, and shipping needs of these early farmers and riverboat operators.

It was the only port in the area until Florence was founded in 1818 on the north bank of the Tennessee River. In its earlier history Florence was sometimes called North Port. These two ports were never thought of as competitors because they mainly served people living on different sides of the river.

As Florence grew larger, South Port gradually became known as South Florence. This was no official name change. The nearest thing to an official name came in 1831, when the U. S. Postal Service established a post office there and used the name South Florence. Early records suggest that Hugh Finley was the first postmaster.

The first steamboat came up the Tennessee River to the Muscle Shoals in 1820. Riverboat service expanded rapidly thereafter. In the 1820's South Port (South Florence) and Florence were the main shipping ports in the Shoals area. South Florence was by far the largest cotton shipping port in North Alabama until the Tuscumbia Landing and the Tuscumbia, Courtland, and Decatur Railroad were established in the early 1830's. During these early years, South Florence had a thriving population with several large warehouses and merchandising establishments.

Paddle Wheeler on the Tennessee

The establishment of the Tuscumbia Landing on the south side of the Tennessee River and then the building of the Tuscumbia, Courtland, and Decatur Railroad in the early 1830's, sounded the death knell of South Florence. With these two developments, cotton planters, business people, and travelers found the railroad and Tuscumbia Landing much more convenient than the wagon roads leading to the unimproved port facilities at South Florence. Many people in South Florence saw the handwriting on the wall. According to one citizen, John R. Price, South Florence literally moved over to Tuscumbia. It is not surprising that in the 1830's South Florence began a slow gradual decline.

After the establishment of local newspapers in Tuscumbia (*The Tuscumbian*) and in Florence (*The Florence Gazette*) small news items often appeared about businesses and people in South Florence. One of the first settlers in South Port was Joseph Heslip, builder of the first iron-making furnace in Alabama. Other prominent names associated with South Port before the Civil War included Robert Black, Hugh Findley, Thomas P. Adams, Edward Jones, and John Johnson.

Apparently no newspaper was ever published in South Florence. Mr. S. C. Posey, editor of the *Florence Gazette* in the 1830's, issued the *South Florence Advertiser* for a brief period as a part of his newspaper.

As the number of steamboats on the Tennessee River increased, they increasingly used the Florence port and Tuscumbia Landings. Apparently South Florence was never incorporated. As a result there was little or no improvement in the port facilities. Neither was there any services rendered the shippers and receivers of commercial products.

Shortly after Florence was established, the Florence Ferry was placed in operation. It traveled from the south end of Court Street in Florence to and from South Florence. In 1832 the Florence Bridge Company was chartered by the legislature. The first permanent bridge across the Tennessee River in the Shoals was completed in 1840. This toll bridge was reworked and strengthened in 1857 by the Memphis and Charleston Railroad so that trains could travel along the branch line from Tuscumbia to Florence. The trains made two trips daily, stopping in South Florence for passengers and cargo.

In 1849 the telegraph cable was strung though the Shoals area and started providing services in South Florence. Also, at least two wagon roads were in common use. One extended eastward while another ran southward though present day Muscle Shoals City.

In the two decades before the Civil War, South Florence continued to experience some change and business activity but could never match the growth that was taking place in Tuscumbia.

Land and Boundary Surveying in North Alabama

The Alabama/Tennessee State Line has a long and interesting history. In the 17th century the king of England issued a colonial charter establishing the Carolinas. The 35th parallel became the southern boundary of North Carolina. When the State of Tennessee was created in 1795, that line became the southern boundary of Tennessee.

The exact location of this line was not important until the Territory of Alabama was created in 1817. From that time forward, Alabama and Tennessee established their own separate system of laws, taxation, government regulations, and services. The exact location of the boundary line became increasingly important over the years.

General John Coffee returned to his home in Tennessee a popular hero after the War of 1812 and resumed his interest in farming, river boating, land speculation, and other such business ventures.

In addition to his other interests, Coffee was also a popular land surveyor. He had helped survey the town of Huntsville in 1809 and some areas in Tennessee. In 1816, through influence of General Andrew Jackson and Representative John Walker, President James Madison appointed Coffee one of the federal surveyors of Alabama. The following year Coffee applied for and was given the position, Surveyor General of Alabama at a salary of $2000 per year.

U.S. Government lands could not be sold to a land-hungry public until they were surveyed. Surveying the land in north Alabama was Coffee's responsibility. The state line had been surveyed westward from Georgia to the northwestern corner of Madison County. Coffee had to locate and finish the state line westward to the Mississippi state line.

In 1817 Coffee led a small army of surveyors, chain bearers, and laborers northward from Huntsville to the state line. A crew started from the northwest corner of Madison County, then proceeded to locate and mark out the state line westward to the northwest corner of Alabama.

Locating and marking out the state line was only the beginning of a much bigger project. As one team of surveyors marked out the state line, others were busy marking out ranges, townships, and sections in northwest Alabama. The first great sale of public land in northwest Alabama was held soon thereafter in Huntsville in 1818.

Many people were eager to get jobs on this surveying project. The work not only paid a good wage but provided the opportunity to locate the best farm land. Many of the workers used this knowledge to buy good land for themselves. They also gave advice to other land purchasers for a fee.

In 1823 Coffee removed the U.S. Land Office from Huntsville to Florence where he had established his home. Coffee remained Surveyor General of Alabama until his death in 1833.

Part Two: The Ante Bellum Period: From Statehood to the Civil War

The Founding of Florence, Alabama

In 1798, shortly after George Washington retired from the Presidency, Congress created the Mississippi Territory. What was later to be Alabama was a part of that territory until March 1, 1817, when Congress created the Alabama Territory.

The land around the Muscle Shoals had been purchased from the Chickasaw and Cherokee Indians in 1816 and Indians still owned about half of what is today Colbert County. Actually, Indians constantly moved about the whole area. While they were not wild savages, neither were they settled responsible citizens. The lands about the Muscle Shoals were relatively unsettled. The census of 1820 showed that only 4,783 inhabitants were then in Lauderdale County. The resources of the area were almost totally undeveloped. The settlers in the area were squatters because the land had not yet, in 1817, been surveyed and put up for sale. In fact, in 1816 shortly after this land was purchased from the Indians, the U.S. Land Office was moved from Nashville to Huntsville where it could best arrange for the survey and sale of the land in the Muscle Shoals area.

This situation offered great opportunity for town builders. There was no shortage of men who recognized this opportunity. In the two years and nine months that Alabama was a Territory and preceding its admission to the Union as a state, at least eight towns were founded on the banks of the Tennessee River between the upper Muscle Shoals and the Mississippi state line. These towns included such names as Bainbridge, Marion, Yorks Bluff, Tuscumbia, Florence, Havana, Savage Springs, and Waterloo.

This outburst of town building in the Muscle Shoals area in 1818 and 1819 was brought on by the belief that a great commercial center would develop at the foot of the Muscle Shoals which was also the head of the navigable portion of the Tennessee River. The founders of Bainbridge in advertising their town stated that Bainbridge was situated at the head of navigation on the Tennessee River. They also claimed that the great bulk of good land lay south of the Tennessee River, which would force the trade up to Bainbridge.

Muscle Shoals When River Was Low

The founders of Florence, in their advertisements, stated

"Intelligent men, from all quarters possessing any tolerable knowledge of the Tennessee River, and that tract of country commonly called the Big Bend, have long foreseen that at the lower end of the Muscle Shoals, there MUST, in the natural course of things, spring up one of the largest commercial towns in the interior of the South-western section of the Union… Florence, therefore, must be the entrepot of groceries and foreign goods for the whole of the upper country of the Tennessee…"

The founders of Florence claimed that they had carefully examined the different sites along the Tennessee River and after comparing their relative advantages and disadvantages, they had unanimously selected the spot best suited for the site of a great commercial town. They also pointed out that Florence was laid out on the northern bank of the Tennessee River, at the foot of the Muscle Shoals, about a mile above the mouth of Cypress Creek and opposite the lower end of a large and beautiful Patton Island.

Florence was founded in Huntsville by land speculators. In February, 1818, a group of Huntsvillians formed the Cypress Land Company. The organizers adopted Articles of Association in which it was stated that the company was founded for the "purpose and intention of laying out a town by the name of Florence and establishing one or more ferries for the public benefit."

The town builders on the frontier were, generally speaking, better educated than the typical frontiersman and they were experienced businessmen. Many of them apparently hoped to expand their business activities and become planters. The town builders usually were men of some wealth and they were also men who had access to investment capital though their acquaintance with others. Finally, the town builders were usually men active in politics or had close ties with government officials. The founders of the Cypress Land Company were typical town builders except for the fact that they were more experienced, better educated, and had far more political power than most town builders.

The trustees of the Cypress Land Company included John Childress and Dabney Morris who were businessmen; Leroy Pope, sometimes called the father of Huntsville, active in business and politics; James Jackson, a planter and state legislator; General John Coffee, a businessman-planter and government surveyor; Thomas Bibb, a businessman and second governor of Alabama; and John McKinley, a businessman, state legislator, national congressman, and finally an Associate Justice of the U.S. Supreme Court. It is doubtful that any other town in Alabama was founded by men with such an array of experience, talent and political influence.

Shortly after the Cypress Land Company was formed, the Trustees purchased 5,515 acres of land at a government land sale for $85,235.24, which amounted to about $15.50 an acre. After the purchase, the trustees arranged for Ferdinand Sannoner and Hunter Peel to plan and lay out the city of Florence.

The trustees felt that they should take some action that would give Florence a better chance for success. To accomplish this, the trustees set aside an entire block for a public park, one for educational purposes, one for a market place, and two acres on the edge of town were set aside for a cemetery. In addition to this, the trustees set aside two lots for a county courthouse and another lot for a jail. They promised to build a courthouse and a jail at Cypress Land Company's expense if Florence was chosen to be the county seat of Lauderdale County. To add further appeal, the trustees promised that the Company would also build a tavern for the town.

By April 1818 they had surveyed eleven streets extending east and west and eleven extending north and south and laid off 412 lots. Almost immediately after the town was planned, the trustees started advertising the town. They planned to hold a great land sale on July 22, 1818.

The planned sale was advertised throughout most of the South and buyers came from great distances. The sale was held in Huntsville. Most men made purchases after examining the plat of the town which was on public display. The sale lasted for several days. When it closed, the Cypress Land Company had sold nearly 300 lots for $223,508.00.

In addition to the well-publicized belief that Florence would surely become a commercial center because it was at the head of the navigation on the Tennessee River, other features persuaded people to buy lots. The town builders confidently predicted that Florence would become the county seat of Lauderdale County. Considering their political influence and the lack of any other town in Lauderdale County at the time, the prediction had real meaning. The founders of Florence also pointed out that the Jackson Military Road extending from Nashville to New Orleans passed through Florence. They also pointed out that twelve months earlier, General Andrew Jackson had recommended that the federal government create an armory and cannon factory in the vicinity of Florence. The founders confidently expected Florence would become an industrial center although this was not stressed as much as the commercial opportunities. It was stated that the surrounding area had large quantities of iron ore, coal, timber, and rich cotton growing soil. The creeks in the vicinity abound with sites for factories that operated with water power, and it was thought that some textile factories would be established in the area to make coarse cotton cloth suited for slave wear.

The founders of Florence tried to convince the purchasers of lots that Florence was already an assured commercial success. Before the sale of lots, the founders announced that two commercial houses importing goods directly from Europe had plans to move their headquarters to Florence within the next year. They also claimed that another group of men were making plans to purchase a steamboat to operate on the Tennessee River. To make the purchase of lots easy, a buyer could play one fourth down and the remainder in three equal annual installments.

The actual building of Florence got underway after the sale of lots in July, 1818. The Cypress Land Company quickly acted to carry out its promises. A tavern was built as promised. Also a ferry crossing the Tennessee River at the south end of Court Street was put into service and the shoreline was cleared so other boats and water craft could conveniently land. In early 1819, the Alabama and East Tennessee Steamboat Company was organized with headquarters in Florence. The directors authorized John McKinley to contract for the purchase of a steamboat not to exceed 100 tons exclusive of machinery. The boat was to draw no more than three feet of water. The first steamboat, the Osage, arrived in Florence in March, 1821. According to a Huntsville newspaper advertisement, the boat brought 500 lbs. of lead, 10,000 lbs of coffee, 8,000 lbs of nails, 40 hogshead of sugar, 30 barrels of mackerel, 30 kegs of white lead, 5 tons of bar iron, and 24 bolts of scotch bagging. This was precisely the type of merchandise the founders of Florence expected to receive and then sell to the surrounding communities.

Florence was chosen as the county seat of Lauderdale County and true to their promise, the trustees of the Cypress Land Company arranged for James Pursell and Nathan Vaught to build a courthouse. It was completed about 1821 and the county jail was completed about a year later. One writer claimed that the courthouse cost $5,700, the jail cost $20,000 and the tavern cost $30,000.

Florence grew in other ways. In 1819, a newspaper, the <u>Florence Gazette</u>, was established and thrived until after the Civil War. A post office was also opened in 1819. In 1820, a school was established on the edge of town by John Coffee. Five years later, a professor, William Spencer Wall, an Episcopal minister, established a school on Cedar Street. While these schools were small and probably continued only for a short time, they established the beginning of Florence as an education center. By 1855, Florence had the Florence Male Academy, the Florence Synodical Female College, and the Wesleyan University.

By 1826, the population of Florence had grown and the business activity in the area had expanded to a point where local government was needed. In that year, the State Legislature incorporated Florence and authorized the establishment of a government for the town. As Florence became self-governing, the Cypress Land Company gradually faded from the scene. But the dynamic imaginative leadership that characterized the founding of Florence continued.

The dream that Florence would become a great commercial center through which merchandise would pass to surrounding towns and through which cotton and other raw materials would be exported to other parts of the world, was dominant in the minds of Florentines long after the founders passed on. Florentines took positive actions to make this dream come true. By 1841, Florence had established a wharf, appointed a wharf master, and established a rate schedule for water crafts of all kinds that wanted to dock at the Florence Wharf. In 1846, a typical year, the wharf master collected the sum of

$246.50 wharfage. This amount was paid by forty steamboats, 3 keel boats, and 4 flatboats. The Florentines also gave their support to road building which would connect Florence to neighboring cities. In 1851, the city agreed to purchase $5,000 worth of stock in a Plank Road Company which would connect Florence with Rogersville and Lawrenceburg, Tennessee. Three years later, the town purchased $10,000 worth of stock in the Nashville and Florence Railroad. While these ventures did not prove successful, they indicate the determination of a frontier town to survive and grow.

Flowing Streams were the Main Source of Power in the 19th Century

Perhaps one can best see the struggle of the Florentines to build a progressive town with dollar figures. In the 1840's and 1850's, Florence contributed $5,000 to building the Florence Female Academy (which was built on the lot that the founders set aside for educational purposes). Nearly $10,000 was contributed to the construction of the Wesleyan Hall which housed the Wesleyan University. Over $15,000 was contributed to the building of roads and railroads into Florence.

It seems obvious that although we may admire the early Indian fighters, the steady yeoman farmers and planters, it was the town builders who brought civilization to the Muscle Shoals area. It was in the towns where educational institutions developed, where newspapers, the post office, and later the telegraph offices were located. Traveling lecturers, traveling shows, and entertainers chose to perform in towns. It was the townspeople who planned and promoted roads and the means of communication. It was in the towns where businessmen mobilized capital, built factories and merchandising establishments. It was the existence of these conditions that make the founders of Florence and other towns the real civilizing influence in the Muscle Shoals area.

Tuscumbia's beginning

In May 1817, a group of U.S. soldiers camped on a hill overlooking the Big Springs in what is today Tuscumbia. At this time there was one store and three dwellings in the area. No town or county existed in the Muscle Shoals area, but changes were coming.

Population was growing rapidly. Florence and other towns were being planned by private land speculators. Many of the early settlers and speculators believed the Big Springs along with the mouth of Spring Creek was a natural town site and would surely become a flourishing city. A letter by Ferdinand Sannoner stated that the springs produced almost as much water as the spring in Huntsville and that Spring Creek afford sufficient water to power manufacturing machinery. Another writer stated that it was a well-known fact that the south side of all rivers in the southern latitude was most healthy.

Still others claimed that the mouth of Spring Creek was an excellent landing and harbor site which would surely develop as a result of the exports and imports of the vast and fertile country to the south and east of the Big Springs.

The settlers and speculators who wanted a town at the Big Springs believed that Florence was a competitor. These settlers claimed that the country and south side of the river was vastly superior to the north side of the river where Florence was located. Also, it was stated that if a town was not established at Big Springs, inhabitants on the south side of the Tennessee River would be forced across the river to Florence even though the south side of the river was superior in quantity of their surplus produce, wealth, and numbers.

A judge in Tennessee, who had an interest in the Shoals Area, wrote that if the land around the Big Springs was sold as city lots rather than "common land", the federal treasury would be greatly enriched. Fear was expressed that if the federal government did not lay out a town and sell the lots, the developers of Florence would buy the land and build a town.

In September, 1818 after Franklin County had been established, several letters were written complaining that President James Monroe had not set aside the Big Springs area as a town site. Actually the area had been designated a town site and withdrawn from public land sales. But no instruction had been given by Washington officials to lay off a town, hence no action had been taken locally.

This delay was caused partially by poor communications but also because some Washington officials believed that another town so close to Florence "would be useless." Some Franklin Countians blamed John Coffee for the delay. They pointed out that he had invested heavily in Florence real estate and planned to make his home there.

Delays notwithstanding, by June, 1819 a town had been laid off at the Cold Water Spring. It seems very likely that Ferdinand Sannoner drew up plans for the town. He was a deputy surveyor employed by the government and had written several letters describing the Big Springs, Spring Creek, and the surrounding area.

The federal government started selling lots at the Cold Water Spring on June 9, 1820. About six months later, on December 20, 1820, the Alabama legislature incorporated the town of Ococoposo, an Indian word referring to cold water. On June 14, 1821, the name was changed to Big Spring and in December, 1822 it was changed to Tuscumbia the name of a Chickasaw chief.

Lauderdale County Named For War Hero

Most counties in Alabama are named for some prominent person. Lauderdale County was named for Lt. Col. James Lauderdale, sometimes referred to as "the gallant Tennessean".

James Lauderdale was born in Virginia. As a child, he moved with his family to Sumner County, Tennessee in 1793. There he grew to manhood in one of the most prominent plantation families in the area. Andrew Jackson and numerous other leading citizens of middle Tennessee were his neighbors.

As a young man, he became a land surveyor and prospered in that profession. He never married. One neighbor expressed the view that his death was a real disappointment to many female hearts who cast hopeful eyes upon this prosperous, mild mannered, southern gentleman.

Shortly after the Creek Indian War started in 1813 with the Fort Mims Massacre in Alabama, General Andrew Jackson called for volunteers to help suppress the Indian uprising. Lauderdale, eager for military action and glory, quickly volunteered. He was elected a major and assigned to a Cavalry Regiment commanded by General John Coffee. A short time later he was promoted to lieutenant-colonel.

Lauderdale suffered a painful wound on November 9, 1813, in the Battle of Talladega. A fellow officer saw him stoically picking particles of shattered bone from the wound. After treatment, he continued on active duty.

James Lauderdale gained favor with General Andrew Jackson. While encamped at Fort Strothers, a large number of Tennessee volunteers, believing their enlistments were expiring, made preparation to return home without proper authority. Lauderdale took it upon himself to persuade them to remain on active duty until the war ended. His speech appealing to their patriotism and self-esteem was in vain; they paid him no heed.

The Creek warriors, commonly known as the Red Sticks, were defeated in the Battle of Horseshoe Bend on March 27, 1814. The Creek War was over. Many of the Tennessee Volunteers returned home but James Lauderdale continued on active duty with General Jackson's army in the New Orleans area.

Just prior to Christmas in 1814 a large British military force moved northward along the Mississippi River toward New Orleans. Jackson sent 1200 men, including Lt. Col.

James Lauderdale, to block the advancing British. After an hour of hand-to-hand combat, both armies withdrew. During this action Lauderdale along with twenty three other Tennesseans was killed. When his body was found, his hand firmly grasped his sword which, according to his friends, demonstrated the courage which had marked the whole of his life.

James Lauderdale was first buried on the battlefield but later reinterred in the New Orleans Protestant Cemetery. He was the highest ranking Tennessean killed in action while serving under General Andrew Jackson's command.

In February 6, 1818, the Alabama Territorial Legislature created Lauderdale County and named it in honor of Lt. Col. James Lauderdale. Both Tennessee and Mississippi also, named counties in honor of this noted officer.

The First Lauderdale County Court House

The county courthouse has always held a unique place in Lauderdale County. Sometimes called the "seat of justice", it is the one public building that most people visit at some time in their life. It has been the symbol of common interests that exist among the people, communities and businesses of Lauderdale County.

When Lauderdale County was created in February 6, 1818, there was no county courthouse. Neither was there a town in the county. The legislature which formed the county specified that the County Commission would temporarily meet at the "Col. Pulsar Place." This place was located some point east of Cypress Creek but near the Creek. The Commissioners had the authority to build a courthouse which could serve as a permanent capital of the county, but there was no agreement on where it should be built.

The founders of Florence helped solve this problem. The land speculators who founded the town of Florence wanted to insure the success of their real estate investment. To attract businessmen and settlers, they set aside tracts of land to be used for churches, a cemetery, a school, and perhaps most important, they agreed to build a tavern. They knew that if Florence became the county seat, this would stimulate the sale of lots and give the frontier town permanence and stability. Therefore, the founders of Florence set aside a "square for a courthouse and a lot for jail." Their advertisement explained that this was done with the belief that Florence would become the seat of justice for the county of Lauderdale. This land set aside for the courthouse was located at the intersection of Tennessee and Court Streets where the County-City Office building is currently located.

There was no opposition to Florence becoming the county seat. The County leaders and the founders of Florence were mainly the same group of people. Also, Florence was near the center of the County which was more convenient to all the people than any other location. Perhaps most important, there was no other town in existence at the time to compete with Florence. In a sense Florence became county capital by default.

Shortly after the first Florence land sale in 1818, the commissioners signed a contract with Mr. James Pursell of Maury County, Tennessee in which he agreed to build the courthouse for Lauderdale County.

Plans for the first courthouse were drawn by William W. Garrard, a Kentuckian who came to the area shortly after Florence was founded. Garrard was elected County

Clerk in 1820 when his fellow Kentuckian, Colonel George Coulter, gave up the position. He continued as County Clerk until 1840.

Despite some delays, Purcell did get the building started in 1821. Unfortunately he became sick with a fever from exposure while searching for runaway slaves. He died October 22, 1821. Before his death, he arranged for Nathan Vaught, also of Maury County, Tennessee to complete the building.

The first Lauderdale County courthouse was completed in 1823. The total cost was $5700. Twenty five hundred was paid in cash and the balance of ($3200) was paid in land located about two miles north of Florence.

The courthouse was two stories high. Each story was sixteen feet high. Ten large columns decorated the front of the building while two large outside stairways on the north and south side of the building led to the second floor. A single front and back door led into the first floor. Numerous large windows, typical of southern architecture, provided light and fresh cool air in the hot summer days before air conditioning and electric lights. At least three large chimneys extended through the roof drawing smoke from several fireplaces.

Perched on top of the courthouse was a large steeple which extended another one and one-half story high. The bottom part of the steeple contained a large clock with four faces looking north, south, east, and west. The numbers on the clock were roman numerals. The hands on all four faces were powered by one timing mechanism which consisted of a complex system of chains, pulleys, and weights.

Records disagree as to who build the original clock and when it was installed. It seems likely that it was built by a Mr. Phemester in Mount Sterling, Kentucky. The county commissioners contracted with him in 1823 to make a clock within seven months.

Apparently this clock, mounted in the steeple of the original courthouse, lasted until 1899 when the new courthouse was built and a new clock was acquired from E. Howard Tower Clock Company of Boston.

Equally if not more important than the clock was the large bell situated in the steeple above the clock. This bell served the Town of Florence in the 1800s much like television, radio, newspapers, and sirens serve Florence today. The sound of the bell communicated important messages to the whole community very quickly. Apparently the bell was connected to the clock and rang at regular intervals. It was rung by hand to announce special occasions such as, fires, curfew, and the beginning of court session. It was also used to call out volunteer firemen and help celebrate occasions in the town.

First Lauderdale County Courthouse with Clock and Bell Tower (Courtesy Robert Steen)

The first courthouse was probably the largest building in Lauderdale County until the 1850s when Wesleyan Hall was completed on the campus of Florence Wesleyan University.

From the very beginning the courthouse served the county in the same way it serves today. It housed county offices and was the place where official County business was transacted. The courtroom stood out as a place of special importance. In addition to regular court proceedings, the County Commission and the Florence Aldermen held regular meetings there. Also the courtroom was used for public lectures, political speeches, public meetings, and other forms of business and public entertainment.

The first courthouse continued in use until 1899 when it was torn down and a new courthouse constructed on the same site.

Life in Early Florence

History is usually told from the point of view of the influential community leaders. This means that the reader is often unable to learn much about the common people. Occasionally there is an outstanding exception. In 1823 Robert Hughes, an ordinary working man was helping build the first courthouse in Lauderdale County. While living in Florence and working on this project, he wrote a letter to his brother, Daniel, in Maysville, Kentucky. The letter provides some interesting insights into the thinking and experiences of a common man in Florence at that early time. The letter has been preserved through the efforts of Mrs. Lois Henderson and Jamie Yancey Loughrey.

Robert Hughes and his brother Daniel, like many young men in that early period of history saw the frontier as an exciting place which offered far more opportunities than the more settled, well-populated communities. These brothers were probably attracted to Florence from Kentucky because their uncle, William W. Garrard lived here. People, young men especially, were highly mobile. Daniel Hughes stayed in Florence a short period of time before moving on to the New Orleans area and a few months later returned to Kentucky. Robert Hughes secured employment helping build the courthouse and remained in Florence.

William Garrard became County Clerk in 1820 and continued to serve in that position until 1840. Later in life he served as Brigadier General commanding the militia.

Robert Hughes wrote that he knew nothing about construction work when he came on the job but quickly learned to do most types of construction work. Garrard drew the plans for the courthouse, and Hughes was proud of the fact that he could understand the drawings. He did several kinds of work on the court house. He made two of the courthouse doors and helped make the other two. He also made four shutters for the windows for which he was paid one hundred dollars and made two of the clock faces and helped make the circular cornice. He wanted the job of framing the steeple, but apparently was denied the opportunity.

Building materials were very scarce on the frontier. Most materials had to be gathered locally. Some manufactured materials such as nails and glass could be brought to Florence in the 1820s only with great difficulty. No good roads existed and the first steamboat came up the Tennessee River while the court house was still under construction. Railroads had not been invented.

Bricks were usually made on the building site while stone and wood materials were gathered from the surrounding areas. Robert Hughes wrote that he and some of his fellow workers went up the Tennessee River about forty miles to Elk River to cut a "raft of planks." They build the raft in the mouth of a small stream that ran into the Elk River about five miles from the Tennessee River. They cut timber and finished their raft late one afternoon and started down river. They intended to stop and camp overnight on the ground at the mouth of the Elk River. But among numerous islands, and in the darkness, they lost their way and got into the swift flowing Tennessee River. Hughes expected the raft to crash as they tried to maneuver it over the Muscle Shoals. But they enjoyed good luck. They landed on a little island, fastened the raft to bushes, and lay on the wet planks all night. They arrived safely in Florence the next day.

Although Hughes seemed to be getting along very well as a worker on the courthouse, he was not happy. He wanted to leave Florence in the spring of 1823 but could not make satisfactory arrangements. Cash was scarce. Very few businessmen would promise cash payments to their "hands". He stated that people lived very "ruff" in early Florence.

Some of the economic difficulties probably resulted from the absence of any banking facilities in the Muscle Shoals area. Despite the hardships, some construction was going on in Florence. William Garrard was just completing a large house. More importantly the beautiful two-story frame house known as "Mapleton" was being built by George Coulter. Coulter, like Hughes and Garrard and many other early settlers in Florence came from Kentucky.

By late summer 1823, Hughes' dream of getting-ahead and finding adventure on the frontier was completely gone. He believed that a person could make money equally as fast in the old country as on the frontier and besides he would see more pleasure.

Hughes' attempt to communicate with other people proved to be a constant problem on the frontier. Mail was delivered very slowly or not at all. Hughes had not received a letter from his brother for over six months although "five or six letter" had been written to the brother. As a result of the bad conditions, letters were often sent "by hand" when possible. Many of the letters written by Hughes were sent by a Mrs. Boggs, a merchant in Florence who made several trips to Kentucky.

Stagecoaches in the Shoals

No one knows when the first stagecoach started serving the Muscle Shoals area. Folklore suggests that stagecoaches might have been traveling between the Shoals area and Huntsville before Alabama became a territory in 1817. We do know that stagecoach travel was common in the area when Alabama became a state in 1819. This kind of business suffered from many problems and small profits, hence service to the Muscle Shoals area seems to have been irregular and not highly dependable for passenger travel and freight hauling during the entire antebellum period.

The Patrick Stagecoach Line was probably one of the last to offer service to the Shoals area. In 1849 Mr. P.F. Patrick announced the opening of a line that would operate between Memphis and Huntsville. Customers were assured that stagecoaches would arrive on schedule, that stagecoaches would offer the utmost comfort, and that each stagecoach would be pulled by four of the finest horses. The stagecoaches were scheduled to leave Memphis for Huntsville and points in between on Monday, Wednesday, and Friday. The east-bound coaches would pass through Harden Springs and Eastport, Mississippi and Florence and Athens, Alabama. Return trips would simply reverse this route. The well-operated stage line stopped every 12 to 15 miles to change horses and for passengers' comfort. Most stagecoaches were built to carry six passengers but it was not unusual for as many as 10 adults to occupy the coach at one time.

It seems that all stagecoach operators claimed to have fine horses. One traveler was appalled when he saw the "small scraggly animals" being hitched to the coach he was to travel in. He was not reassured when he learned that one of the lead horses was named "Eclipse".

It also seems that all stagecoach owners advertised that their coaches had fine upholstery and offered great comfort. Travelers did not always find this to be true. Under the best conditions passenger travel on stagecoaches was an ordeal to be endured not a pleasure ride to be enjoyed. In the early days the ever present threat of Indians and outlaws, bad roads, and unpleasant companions all made up a travel experience filled with hardship and danger. It was a common practice – when ruts were deep, the road was sandy and boggy, rivers flooded, or hills were steep, – for passengers to be invited to get out and walk. This tended to ensure greater safety for the passengers and rested the horses from their strenuous efforts.

One traveler, preparing himself for a trip across Alabama by stagecoach, provided himself with a pocket flask of good brandy and a stone jug of good sherry wine. These liquid refreshments often referred to and thought of as medicine, were supplemented with a pound of bologna sausage and a quantity of crackers. As protection against the cool night air, he took a "comfort" which was described as "cotton wadded between calico."

Travelers quickly discovered there was simply no defense against the crudities of fellow passengers. One stagecoach was filled beyond capacity with eight passengers which included two women (one never spoke and the other never shut up), two children, one man who was miserably ill with the "colicky", and two "negro dealers", one of whom "was deaf as a post." This latter passenger was described as an inveterate smoker, with a nasty, vulgar, and obscene wit and poetry of the day, which he did not hesitate to repeat at all times without much regard to company.

One stagecoach after a night of travel, stopped for breakfast at a "sorry cabin... in a scanty clearing" where a traveler paid fifty cents for a breakfast consisting of "poor coffee, hominy, – hog in several shapes such as sausages, spare ribs and pickled chine – and Indian bread." This early morning fare was served at a table situated in a violent draft from the open door.

One critic of frontier foods felt real contentment when the stagecoach stopped for dinner at an established Inn where the food was "tolerable" but the environment not much improved. The local diners who shared a table with him were all "cotton worshippers", who talked of nothing else, thought of nothing else, and no doubt dreamt of nothing but long and short staple and twenty cents a pound.

The suffering stagecoach travelers could look forward to better things, and apparently the Patrick Stagecoach Line did not last long. By 1849 travel by steamboat from Florence and Tuscumbia to Memphis and other points along the Mississippi and Ohio Rivers was common. Also, the Memphis and Charleston Railroad was nearing completion through North Alabama and Mississippi. The horse-drawn vehicles were being rapidly replaced by what was then modern technology.

David Crockett in the Shoals

David Crockett, one of the best-known men in American History, never lived in the Muscle Shoals area but was closely associated with northwest Alabama.

Crockett first became acquainted with Alabama territory during the Creek Indian War 1813-1814. When General Andrew Jackson called for volunteers to put down the Indian uprising, Crockett was eager to enlist. His wife, however, raised strong objections which Crockett ignored. He later wrote "I always had a way of just going ahead at whatever I had a mind to do."

As a soldier in Jackson's army, Crockett crossed the Tennessee Valley several times and fought in most of the major battles during the war. He also gained much knowledge of the land and resources in Alabama while serving as a spy. He was well acquainted with the forest and the ways of the Indians, hence he was often called upon to locate and follow major groups of Indians. This military service carried him into all parts of Alabama.

At the end of the war, the Creek Indians ceded to the U.S. government a large tract of land. The "Great Migration" of white settlers into Alabama began quickly thereafter.

Crockett with some close friends made several trips into Alabama to search out good land on which to settle. On one occasion he got separated from his friends and became seriously ill with "agues and fevers." On this occasion he fully expected to die but was nursed back to health by friendly Indians and settlers.

In 1816 the Chickasaw Indians signed a treaty ceding much of their land in southern Tennessee and northwest Alabama to the U.S. government. The following year, Crockett chose to settle on land located on the head waters of Shoal Creek in what is today known as David Crockett State Park in Tennessee. Geographically, he was closely connected to the Muscle Shoals area although neither Lauderdale County nor Florence had been created at that time.

Crockett cleared a small farm and with $3000 of borrowed money, built a grist mill, a large distillery, a powder mill and a blacksmith shop. He also acquired some slaves and some good livestock.

It could be argued that bad luck followed Crockett. Many of his endeavors ended in failure through no fault of his own. In 1821 a quick unexpected flood hit the Shoal

Creek. People at the time called the flood "a great fresh" and great it was. All the industries and improvements Crockett had made on his land were swept away. He was left with some land, heavy debts he could not pay, and little else.

Like many frontiersmen, Crockett felt the need for "more elbow room." He gave all his property to his creditors and made a new start in northwest Tennessee.

After moving away from the Shoal Creek, Crockett gained national prominence as a frontiersman, bear hunter and national congressman. By 1836 when he was killed at the Alamo in Texas, he was one of the best-known men in the U.S.

Bear Hunting on the Frontier

Hunting was a part of American Frontier way of life. Bear hunting had a special appeal. Little has been written about bear hunting in the Muscle Shoals area because most of the bears had been "hunted out" by the time the settlers arrived in the area.

Bears were hunted for several reasons. Of course sport was of major importance. But on the frontier there was often little difference between sporting activity and essential labor. The hunter who killed a four or five hundred pound bear was the proud owner of a thick pelt that could serve as a blanket, mattress, coat, or several other purposes. He also had enough meat to last his family through a cold winter. On one occasion a Limestone County settler welcomed a visitor into his cabin by giving him a bearskin spread on the floor to sleep on and a bundle of squirrel and coon skins to serve as a pillow.

Bears were also hunted for protection. Bears were destructive and dangerous. In the early 1820s, a bear tore down a rail fence while entering a cane patch and then destroyed about 400 square feet of ripe sugar cane. The farmer joined with neighbors to hunt and kill the bear. Bears were notorious for breaking into chicken houses, smokehouses, and other buildings where food, especially honey and syrup, was stored. It was not unknown for bears to kill cows, hogs, and other livestock.

Hunting bears was one of the most dangerous sports. A good pack of trained dogs, a well-primed rifle and a sharp knife were essential to success. More than a few hunters carried scars proving that the bear could be a deadly adversary.

The English settlers in America were familiar with bears. Bear baiting was a common sporting activity in England in the 17th and 18th century. That same practice was continued in America. When a bear was captured, which was unusual, the animal was sometimes chained to a tree with enough freedom to move about and defend himself. Then a pack of dogs was turned loose to attack the bear. The fight between the bear and the dogs often continued for several hours. A larger bear could kill a dog with one vicious stroke of his paw. In the fight some dogs almost inevitably were killed and others injured for life. But several dogs attacking from all sides could usually wear out the energy of the largest bear. In any event the bear was killed at the end of the fight.

David Crockett is one of the few Americans who gained great fame as a bear hunter. It is claimed that he once killed 26 bears in one day and over 600 bears in one year in western Tennessee. Crockett is also noted for killing one of the largest bears in the Southeast, an animal that weighed over 650 pounds.

There was real danger and hardship associated with bear hunting. Therefore the typical frontiersman usually left bear hunting to others except where the bear posed a threat to life and property.

Marquis de Lafayette, American Hero Remembered in the Shoals

The name "LaGrange" is familiar to most people in the Muscle Shoals area. That is not surprising since the name LaGrange has been a part of local history for about 200 years.

Most people would connect the name "LaGrange" with the old LaGrange College site, while others may think of LaGrange Hall on the UNA campus. Still others would think of LaGrange Living Historical Association which sponsors the Recall LaGrange Festival each year.

Marquis de Lafayette was a French nobleman, who after being kicked out of the French army in the 1770's, offered his services to General George Washington during the American War for Independence. He was assigned the rank of general and commanded the American forces that captured the British army in the final battle of the war, the Battle of Yorktown.

Lafayette emerged from the American Revolutionary War as one of America's greatest hero's. Despite his noble rank, he was then and has remained in the minds of Americans as a great fighter for liberty and freedom.

About forty years after the American Revolution, General Lafayette was invited to return to the United States as a guest of the nation he helped to form. He came into and toured through the southern part of Alabama at a cost of $6000 to the state. On this tour he often stated that Georgia and Alabama reminded him of his estate near Paris, France, which was known as LaGrange.

While touring Alabama, the "Old General" never came to the Muscle Shoals but his name and the name of his estate was adopted for common usage.

A few months after Lafayette traveled on to Mississippi and other parts of the nation, the Methodist Church created a committee with instructions to choose a site and create a college in northwest Alabama. The college was located in the northeastern part of Franklin County and given the name LaGrange College. A local girls' school in the same area was given the name Lafayette Academy. Also, streets and clubs were named after the "Old General." Thus Lafayette left his mark in the Muscle Shoals without ever coming near the area.

Americans are often accused of having short memories. Not so with General Lafayette. It is reported that during World War One when American troops landed in France to help them fight the German invaders, General John J. Pershing, Commander of the American Expeditionary forces, waved his sword and cried "Lafayette, we are here."

Marquis de Lafayette is well remembered as a fighter for liberty and freedom in his own country. He is sometimes given credit for writing France's Declarations of the Rights of Man and is greatly loved by his fellow Frenchmen.

A bronze statue of Lafayette stands in the central circle of LePuy, his home town. During World War II, the Germans tried to remove this symbol of freedom but found it too heavy. While the Germans waited for heavy equipment to effect the removal, a large group of French Freedom Fighters removed the statue and buried it in a nearby barn. After the war, the Fighters who labeled themselves "Le Group Lafayette, Liberateur du Puy" marched to the barn, dug up the statue and returned it to its proper place of honor.

As a part of the United States bicentennial in 1976, a full size bronze copy of the statue was made and placed on permanent loan in this country.

Probably no names in the entire Muscle Shoals area symbolizes liberty and freedom quite as much as "Lafayette" and "LaGrange".

John McKinley, One of Florence's Most Noted Citizens

John McKinley is one of the most popular historic figures connected with the Muscle Shoals area. He is remembered mainly as one of the three Associate Justices of the U.S. Supreme Court from Alabama. No book length biography, and few records exist to reveal his character or guide a student through his contributions to Alabama history.

McKinley was born May 1, 1780, in Culpepper County, Virginia but spent most of his early life in Lincoln County, Kentucky where his mother's family was prominent in politics. As a young boy, he secured a good education. He read law and was admitted to the bar in 1800 at the age of 19 or 20.

As a promising young lawyer in Louisville, Kentucky, McKinley developed a good law practice and took an active interest in politics and business. He also married and established a family.

Sometime about 1818 or 1819, McKinley moved his family to Huntsville, Alabama. At that time North Alabama was wide open, unsettled, offering great opportunities for energetic men and women to bring civilization, culture and prosperity to the frontier.

We don't know when McKinley became interested in the Muscle Shoals area. In early 1818, he along with General John Coffee, Andrew Jackson and several land speculators, organized the Cypress Land Company which was founded in the city of Florence. When the first big land sale was held in 1818, he bought at least twelve lots in Florence.

When Alabama became a state in December 1819, several new governmental positions were created. He wrote to a friend in Congress, "I am at length a citizen of Alabama and I got here just in time to run for judge." He was defeated. While accepting defeat graciously, he expressed the opinion that his opponent "knows neither law or anything else." But McKinley was most complimentary of the newly formed state legislature saying that the members were "wise, well informed and honest," an opinion that was not widely shared at the time.

After moving to Huntsville, McKinley was either in or trying to get in a public office throughout the remainder of his life. Between 1820 and 1836 he was elected to the Alabama House of Representatives three times, the U.S. House of Representatives two times, and the U.S. Senate two times.

While serving in the U.S. Senate, probably about 1828, McKinley moved from Huntsville to Florence where he had many close friends and some business interest. He built and lived in a large three story brick mansion overlooking the Tennessee River. The house was situated at the northwest corner of the intersection of Veterans (formerly Spring Street) Drive and Seminary Street. The house later burned.

While Florence was his home, McKinley introduced a bill in the U.S. Senate to appropriate public land to pay for the improvement of navigation on the Tennessee River. This bill eventually became a law. The land was sold and the money used to build the first canal around the Muscle Shoals. Also, while living in Florence, McKinley served as a Trustee for the newly created University of Alabama.

In 1836 McKinley was elected to the U.S. Senate for a second term, but that position was not his real goal. He wanted an appointment to the U.S. Supreme Court. Typically, he sought and gained the support of his many powerful friends.

But all their efforts seemed to fail when President Martin Van Buren appointed Judge William Smith of Huntsville, former senator from South Carolina, to the Supreme Court. Surprisingly, the seventy-five year old Smith refused the appointment. It was then offered to McKinley, who accepted immediately. In January 9, 1838, McKinley took his seat as Associate Justice of the Supreme Court. He continued in this position until his death in 1852.

Shortly after his appointment, McKinley moved back to Louisville, Kentucky, where he had lived a major part of his life and where many friends and relatives, including a daughter and a son, lived.

Women on the Muscle Shoals Frontier

Women played a significant part in converting the unsettled Muscle Shoals area into a well-populated, civilized region during the first half of the nineteenth century. During that period women were greatly appreciated as women, but never held leadership positions in antebellum society.

When the Tennessee Valley became a part of the Mississippi Territory by an act of Congress in 1798, there were very few settlers, men or women, in the Muscle Shoals area. That situation changed rapidly. By 1850 Alabama had a white male population of over 219,000 and a white female population of just over 215,000. In addition, by 1850 338,000 black slaves lived in Alabama.

During the entire antebellum period, the number of white men far exceeded the number of white women. In Alabama every county except three had more men than women. On an average, there were about 95 white females to every 100 white males. The Muscle Shoals area was typical. In 1850 Franklin County had 5,524 white females and 5,874 white males while Lauderdale County had 5,479 white females and 5,618 white males. The town of Florence was also typical; in 1850 the white population consisted of 498 males and 399 females.

The smaller number of women on the unsettled area of the frontier can be explained in several ways. Throughout history, men have led the way into new unexplored unsettled areas of the world, and women and children followed. Also, the death rate of women exceeded men. This was due primarily to deaths during childbirth and the total lack of medical treatment for "female problems." In the age group above thirty, there were about eighty five white women to every one hundred white men. Prior to the Civil War there was practically no medical assistance for women if any kind of female problems developed. Midwives usually gave assistance during childbirth. They usually had limited knowledge and experience.

The small ratio of women to men had a definite influence. Females were courted and often married at a very early age. Widows were almost always courted and received marriage proposals. Some cases have been recorded where the widow received a marriage proposal before her dead husband was buried. Of course then perhaps as today, if the widow was young, good looking, and heir to an estate, she attracted more attention.

Also, among slaves and free blacks, men outnumbered women in the Muscle Shoals area. In 1850 there were approximately 3,004 black females to 3,071 males in Lauderdale County; there were 4,035 black females to 4,177 males in Franklin County.

Although females were appreciated by men and society in general, they did not hold leadership positions in any branch of society. Women did not vote, hence they held no elective offices in any of the city or county governments. Women were often present at political meetings and sometimes participated in a ceremonial capacity. But their participation and influence were minimal.

The same was true with appointed positions. Women did not serve on public boards and commissions. The Board of Trustees for LaGrange College, Florence Wesleyan University, and the Florence Female Synodical College were all men, and all the faculty were male except at the female college. Also, women did not become lawyers, medical doctors, dentists, ministers, military leaders, or serve in law enforcement. Women were teachers of children in public and private schools in the 1850s. But the teaching of children was more closely identified with home and motherhood than with professional education.

These patterns of behavior have changed some but not greatly during the last 150 years. A study conducted in the 20th century revealed that state Boards and Commissions in Alabama were made up of 72 percent white men, 19 percent white women, and 3 percent black women. Women make up less than 10 percent of the legislature. Our heritage from the antebellum past is powerful and rich in diversity but it is not always characterized by justice and fairness.

Early Education for Young Ladies in the Shoals Area

In Alabama before the Civil War, most education was practical, and learning took place in the home. Adults assumed that children would grow up and live in a world much like the one they were born into. Therefore, mothers taught their daughters what they needed to know to be mothers and women. Fathers taught their sons how to perform in a "man's world."

Education started and ended for most children in the home. Many parents saw no need for academic education. Others did not have money to pay tuition at private schools and still others simply had no schools to attend. No public school system existed in Alabama until 1854.

Before 1854, most schools were private. For example, in 1840 a Mrs. Thompson of Florence taught school in her home for "small children." In 1850 the Rev. Jonathan B. T. Smith, pastor of the Episcopal Church, advertised that he was opening a female school in his home. The school term was to be five months and tuition was set at $8 a term. In 1860, one year before the Civil War began, Mrs. A. M. Warren opened a private school in her home in Florence for "young ladies and little girls."

In areas where private schools did not exist, community leaders sometimes took the initiative and organized a school for their children. These schools were supported mainly by tuition, although some received a little money from the sale of public land which had been set aside for educational purposes. A school of this nature was organized in the Nauvoo community of Franklin County in the 1850s. The school had about eighteen students and parents paid a fee for each child directly to the teacher on an installment plan. The students were of all ages and included one girl older than the teacher. Collecting tuition was a problem which led the young male teacher to earn extra money by clerking in a store and writing letters and documents for people who could not write. He also read letters for those who could not read.

These beginning students generally learned how to read, write, and do simple arithmetic. In some cases, teachers also taught music, piano, drawing, etc.

By the 1850s the public school movement which had started in the 1830s in New England had spread to Alabama. The Alabama Legislature through the efforts of men like Robert M. Patton of Lauderdale County passed the Public School Act of 1854. This act created the first statewide public school system in Alabama. Although some tuition fees still had to be paid, it put academic education within reach of most white boys and girls in the State of Alabama. It also opened the door of the new teaching profession to women, and thereby created many new jobs for women outside the home.

Apparently these opportunities for students were not greatly appreciated. In 1858-59 in all of Alabama 98,274 children registered for admission to the public schools but the average daily attendance was only about 42,000.

Conditions in the Muscle Shoals area were typical of the entire state. Franklin County had 2,606 students attending eighty schools which operated about five and one-half months each year. Lauderdale County had only 2,255 students registered for fifty seven schools. Average attendance was 977 in Franklin County and 1,058 in Lauderdale County. From these figures it is obvious that only about 40 percent of the children eligible to attend school were actually in school, and most of these had very irregular attendance.

Apparently very few parents gave any consideration to educating their children beyond the basic level in reading, writing, and arithmetic.

Women Were Major Providers for the Family

History has traditionally pictured the male head of the household as the breadwinner, the person who satisfied the material needs of the family. For the well-to-do wife/mother this was not an unrealistic view. But, for the middle and lower class families, it was almost pure myth.

Married women were major providers for the needs of the typical household. When eating time came, the family members looked to the mother, not the father. The wife/mother provided food by planting and maintaining a garden and orchard. She operated the dairy which provided milk, butter, and cheese, and she produced poultry for meat and eggs. She assisted with butchering animals. Much time was spent preserving vegetables and fruits in summer for use in winter.

Women Produced Goods for the Family in the Home

Women provided nearly all the family clothing by spinning, weaving, knitting, and sewing in what was often called "her spare time." Also, the typical housewife usually produced household necessities such as candles, soap, quilts, and other items. It is no exaggeration to state that if women in the home had not produced and preserved food, made clothes, and other common household items, a major portion of the needs of the family simply would not have been met.

A few women worked in the home to earn extra income for their family. For example, several women in the Nauvoo community of Franklin County in the 1850s knitted socks and sweaters and made other items which were sold or traded to local merchants. In Florence at least two women contracted with the town of Florence to provide food and lodging for the town slaves, mules, and horses. They also made clothes for the slaves and harnesses for the mules and horses.

In theory there was a strong healthy, knowledgeable, responsible man at the head of every household. Unfortunately during the pre-Civil War times in the Muscle Shoals area, neither nature nor human society could adequately satisfy this need. The census reports of 1850 and 1860 indicate that most Alabama counties had from nine to thirteen percent of the households headed by women. Lauderdale County was typical. In 1850 Lauderdale County had 1,892 households of which 170 or 9.5 percent were headed by women. Ten years later in 1860 there were 1,981 households in Lauderdale County of which 273 or 12.3 percent were headed by women.

For all practical purposes these women were forced to assume the responsibilities normally performed by the wife and the husband.

Very few of these women became heads of households by giving birth to illegitimate children. The great majority of them were widows.

Because the majority of women were merely housewives, most census takers did not list an occupation for most women. Based on limited data, it appears that over fifty percent of the female heads of households were farmers.

A small number of women did find jobs outside the home. The census of 1850 listed carding, spinning, weaving, sewing, cooking, and washing as occupations in which women were engaged. The 1860 census list of occupations held by women had expanded to include teaching, baking, planting, and factory (textile) working.

Wages for Women Were Low and Discriminatory

There were very few industrial jobs available for men or women in Alabama before the Civil War.

The Globe Factory, established in Florence in 1839 by James Martin and others, was a textile factory employing whole families. In 1850 this factory paid stockholders a 50 percent return on their investments which suggest that labor cost was rather low.

The few women who did work in factories as individuals outside the family unit in the 1850s found wages to be low and discriminatory. Most of the factory working women were single and ranged in age between twelve and twenty. In the 1850s the wages paid to women factory workers ranged between six and twelve dollars per month. The wages paid most women were concentrated at the lower end of the wage scale.

Not only were the wages low, they were usually discriminatory. In 1850 the Foster, Simpson and Company in Lauderdale County employed thirty men and thirty women. While the nature of the work performed is not known, the men were paid an average monthly wage of $10 while the women were paid an average of $7 a month. Joseph Bradford's cotton mill in Coosa County employed eight men and twenty-eight women in 1850. The male employees were paid an average of $12 per month while the women workers averaged $6 per month. G. E. Allen and Brother operated a cotton factory in Marion County in 1860 employing eight men and fourteen women. The male workers were paid an average of $14 per month while the women averaged $6 per month.

These discriminatory rates were typical across the entire state of Alabama. In 1850 the average male textile factory worker was paid $11.71 per month while the average wage for female workers was $7.98 a month.

There were several possible explanations for the low and discriminatory wages for women. Numerous women were eager to get a job even if the wages were low. Also it should be noted that wages of female factory workers compared favorably with other types of women's work. For example, domestic servants were generally paid about $1.50 per month plus room and board.

Women played a much larger role in other economic affairs in the Muscle Shoals area. Women, married and single, became teachers in public and private schools and on the college level. Others owned property and operated their own businesses. It was common for women to operate boarding houses, inns, taverns, dress shops, and other such establishments. Women sometimes bought and sold property. In 1818 when land in Franklin County was put on sale by the national government, at least two women immediately bought land. Later when the Chickasaw Indians were moved westward and the vacated land in western Franklin County was put up for sale, four women purchased land in the Cedar Creek region. In 1856 what we know as "Pope's Tavern" was sold to Sarah M. Gookin. Also, women were often appointed to legal positions. For example Probate Judge W. T. Hawkins in Lauderdale County appointed Kiziah Farmer to be administrator of the estate of William Farmer.

While the lives of the great majority of women centered around home and family, females also played a significant though inferior role in the social and economic world outside the home.

Women's Life Centered Around Home and Family

In the nineteenth century, young women were expected to marry, become mothers, and live out their lives in the home environment. In fact, the most important way a young female could improve her economic quality of life and find happiness was through marriage. Few alternatives were available.

To achieve a good marriage, young ladies received advice from many sources. The local newspapers often printed articles describing how to find a good husband. One piece of advice was given in the <u>Florence Gazette</u> as follows: "When you see a young man modest and retiring in his manners, who cares less about dress than moral character, depend upon it ladies he will make an excellent husband. If you get the one that is kind and attentive to his mother, affectionate to his sister, industrious in his habits, and economical in his business, rest assured you have found one of whom you will never be ashamed."

These articles indirectly gave advice to men. Some were more explicit. One such article stressing the value of modesty, the <u>Florence Gazette</u> stated, "We love a modest unassuming young man wherever we find him: in a counting room, or a law office... or in the pulpit... When in the company with others, he does not usurp all the conversation and endeavor to call the attention of others to himself by boisterous language."

Once a young lady found and married the right man, her legal position and worldly responsibilities changed drastically. When marriage occurred, the young wife's legal identity passed to her husband. While he did not own her body or her property, he could and did control, command, and use both for his purposes. Usually the husband made decisions about where the family would live, how the family income and wealth would be used, and what activities the family would engage in. It would be an exaggeration to say that the wife lived out her life at the beck and call of her husband, but in practice that was the case when the husband chose to exercise his full authority in the marriage relationship.

Woman's role and responsibilities were almost exclusively in the home. Within the home and family, the typical women performed four basic functions. She was wife, mother, servant, and family provider.

Women's Life and Work Centered in the Home and Family

As a wife she was expected to be a helpmate, lover, loyal companion, and a source for moral strength and comfort to her husband. She was expected to give birth to her husband's children and then care for their needs and instill in them socially acceptable values.

Most women in the middle and lower income group were servants in the home to their own families. From early morning to late at night, the typical married woman was busy preparing food, washing dishes, cleaning the house, washing clothes, and performing numerous other chores about the home. She is also the family nurse. It was generally thought that her natural qualities of tenderness and compassion made her a natural nurse. It was also generally believed that men were too rough and insensitive for this kind of work.

Women not only cared for their family, they were usually the primary caretakers for slaves, pets, and other small sickly animals about the home. Her work as servant and nurse was usually constant, repetitious, unrewarding drudgery. It is not surprising that this kind of activity bore the ignoble title "woman's work."

Higher Education for Women in the Shoals

Parents who wanted their daughters to proceed beyond the basic reading, writing, and arithmetic, usually sent them to academies. Privately owned academies operated for boys and girls separately in the larger towns of Alabama. The Muscle Shoals area had at least three academies: the Tuscumbia Female Academy, the Florence Female Academy, and the Locust Dell Academy.

The Locust Dell Academy was on Morrison Avenue in Florence where Willingham Hall on the UNA campus is now located. It was operated by Nicholas Marcelluis Hentz and his wife, Caroline, from 1834 to 1843. This boarding school attracted young ladies from all over the South. During its most prosperous year, this school had about 100 students. The Florence Female Academy operated in the 1840s and 1850s in a building situated on the present site of the U.S. Post Office. Like the Tuscumbia Female Academy, it attracted students mainly from the local area. The Tuscumbia Academy was located on the present site of the Presbyterian Manse.

The families of the students attending these academies were reasonably well-to-do. The educational programs offered by these institutions were designed to make the students into cultured "young ladies" with a smattering of academic training.

In 1855 through the efforts of Rev. W. W. Mitchell, Robert M. Patton, and other prominent members of the Presbyterian Church, the Florence Synodical Female College was established. The Board of Trustees consisted of seventeen men and six women. The school year was made up of two five-month terms. Expenses for room, board, tuition and other fees usually ran about $145 for one term.

The opening of a female college in the Muscle Shoals area added strength to a debate long in progress, about the value of educating females. The negative arguments were often made that women were going to spend their lives as housewives and mothers and therefore did not need an education above the very basic reading, writing, and arithmetic. Others advanced the belief that the female brain did not have the toughness and stamina necessary for higher education.

In June 1850 the Dialectical Society at LaGrange College in Franklin County debated the question "Should females be educated as highly as the males?" The competition was furious. The final decision of this debate was in the affirmative, but naturally this did not settle the matter.

The value of female education remained an open question at least until 1872. The Florence Wesleyan University had ceased to operate during the Civil War and was unable to return to normal operation after the war. The buildings and grounds were given to the Alabama Board of Education which opened the Florence Normal School in these facilities in 1872. The two-year teacher-training institution was the first permanent normal school and the first coeducational institution in the state of Alabama. The training of men and women in the same classroom and with the same standards was looked upon as a major experiment. The female students quickly demonstrated their abilities to cope and to compete with the boys.

Advice for Rural Women in the 19th Century

In the early 19th century about 90 percent of the people in the Muscle Shoals area and the whole nation lived on farms. Life was hard. Every member of the family had to work. Under the difficult conditions, it was almost impossible for women to maintain good health, good looks, and even good manners and morals.

At that period of history, there were very few medical and cosmetic products for women to use, but there was no shortage of advice. While the advice was plentiful, cheap, and usually worthless, it did give some insights into the hardships that women experienced.

Women like men had to do a lot of hard physical labor. As a result, the hands of many women were stiff and hard. They were advised to put on gloves when hoeing and raking. The same advice applied when cooking with skillets, pots, pans, or kettles.

It was claimed that when a woman's hands were "rough and hard," she was unable to feel small articles such as needles or soft and tender objects. As a result, women sometimes could not sew and quilt properly. One writer assured the young women that hard, rough hands are "not so good to hold a baby or dress a wound."

In other words, if a woman had hard, rough hands, she could not perform the work that women were expected to perform. Hence every woman living in the country was urged to knit herself a pair of woolen gloves and wear them.

Women were advised not to forget their faces. It was claimed that many country girls at sixteen "had a complexion of alabaster" and at the age of twenty-six their faces looked "like a runnet bag that had hung six weeks in the chimney corner." An explanation given for the hard, unpleasant complexion was that women "do not wear a bonnet to protect themselves from the sun." Perhaps equally important was the women's habit of "baking their faces before a wood fire." Large numbers of rural mid-19th century women had to cook before a hot open fire in a fireplace or around a very hot stove. One writer claimed that women who cooked before such fires, seldom made any "attempt to shield their faces." And as a result "their brains were as well stewed as the chicken in the pot." Readers of that era were assured that for these reasons, "women grow old, withered, and wrinkled fifteen years before their time."

Appearances were always a source of concern for women. One writer claimed that "Thousands of beautiful blooming country girls make old sallow faced women of themselves before they are thirty by drinking coffee, smoking tobacco, and eating hot bread." The young women were assured that it was as much "a sin for women to get old, brown withered faces, by eating too much as it was for men to get red noses by drinking too much."

Health was then as today, a source of major concern and the subject of much advice and speculation. It was argued that country girls ate more "rich foods than those who lived in the city," and for that reason, even with their country fresh air, their average life span was only a little greater than that of the city folks. According to some thinking of the time, rural women shortened their lives by "living too well and eating too much hot bread and meat." These practices shortened their lives "about as much as city ladies with their fashionable follies."

One writer confidently wrote, "The woman who roasts her head at the fire, disorders her blood, brings on headaches, which injuries her health, and makes her face look like a piece of leather; when she swallows hot coffee, hot bread, greasy victuals and strong pickles, she destroys her stomach, rots her teeth, shortens her life, and makes herself too ugly for any use except scaring the crows off the corn."

Schools in early Tuscumbia

When the first settlers moved into the Big Springs area of Franklin County, which later became known as Tuscumbia, they brought with them a deep appreciation for education. Unfortunately at the time there was no system of public education in Alabama. The education of children was left almost entirely to the parents. In such frontier environment, parents often worked together to establish private schools to meet their needs.

By 1826, Tuscumbia had made much progress. Although the town was only six years old and had a population of about 1,000, there were four schools in operation.

The federal government had given the 16th section of land in each township to the State to be used for educational purposes. The schools established with this land grant were often referred to as a "section or free school." This land grant did provide some free schools but most had to charge a small tuition. Most section schools operated only a short time. The "section school" in Tuscumbia was "crowded with children" in 1826. We have no information about the curriculum, but in all probability it consisted mainly of reading, writing, and arithmetic and other such activities as was appropriate for the beginning child.

A private female school was also operating in Tuscumbia in 1826. It was conducted by "a gentleman" as a private business and without any financial community support. Schools of this type were usually conducted in the teacher's home and were designed to serve the needs of younger children who were just beginning their formal education. Parents of students paid a tuition fee which covered the teacher's salary and other school expenses.

Two academies were organized to serve the needs of older and more advanced children of Tuscumbia. Apparently the Tuscumbia Female Academy was the largest school in Tuscumbia. It was opened on March 1, 1825 by the efforts of several prominent citizens who believed their daughters should be educated as well as their sons. Four trustees including Alex A. Campbell, William H. Whorton, John Hogun and T. Woolbridge were selected by the interested citizens to organize and operate the school. These trustees employed a Miss Farrington to actually supervise the day to day operations of the academy.

Operating money came mainly from student tuition, therefore a fairly large number of tuition paying students were necessary to support the academy. To attract students, an advertisement for the Female Academy was placed in <u>The Tuscumbian</u>. It was aimed at the people all across north Alabama and southern Tennessee. The long advertisement concluded with a notice requesting other editors in other cities to place this ad in their papers and send the bill to the trustees.

The trustees assured interested parents that the academy would be inferior to no other institution in the south or west. The curriculum seems to bear this out. The young ladies were expected to study natural and moral philosophy, history, chemistry, literature, Italian, geography, painting, music, grammar, and "all the lower branches of an English education."

To care for out-of-town students a "suitable and convenient boarding house" with "commodious rooms" was attached to the academy. Room and board were $37.50 for a term which lasted about 4 and one-half months. The Trustees eagerly pointed out the advantages of the Tuscumbia Female Academy. They claimed the tuition was very low and that the town of Tuscumbia offered "a healthy environment" and "a good society."

The Female Academy got off to a good start. It was immediately crowded with "an enrollment of thirty to forty young ladies."

The Tuscumbia Male Academy was opened about this same time but apparently did not enjoy as much early success as the female academy. These academies were totally separate although both were governed by the same trustees except a R.B. Marshall was added to the male academy trustees. A Mr. Moran was employed to superintend and operate the academy.

Courses taught in the male academy were not advertised but the trustees promised that the boys entrusted to Mr. Moran's care would receive "a complete academical course." To insure learning and proper advancement, at the end of each term the students were given an oral public examination.

The advantages of the male academy also included "low tuition" and inexpensive board although no boardinghouse was attached to the school. The "healthy environment" and "good society" in Tuscumbia was also stressed in the advertisements.

Neither of these academies received any financial assistance from the state or federal government. Tuition was the main source of operating capital. Some additional assistance was available in the form of gifts, tax exemptions, and monies raised by the public lottery.

While much is not known about these early schools in Tuscumbia, we can draw some reasonable conclusions. This evident interest in education certainly made Tuscumbia one of the most progressive towns in northwest Alabama in the early 19th century. Also that interest in education probably had some influence in persuading the Methodist Church to locate LaGrange College in Franklin County. Deep seated community values change very slowly. The desire for good schools felt so strongly by the Tuscumbians in the 1820s is still very evident today.

Bibles in Early Tuscumbia

The belief in the Holy Bible led to the organization of the Tuscumbia Bible Society in November 1825, when the town was about five years old. Leaders in the Tuscumbia Bible Society were Dr. A. A. Campbell, David Keller, Joshua Prout, Branham Merrill, James Elliot, Dr. Joseph Prout, J. Barckley, C. C. Macey, William H. Wharton, William Clay, and R. E. Marshall. The objective of the Society was to encourage the "circulation and reading of God's holy word" by ensuring that a "Bible and Testament" was in every home.

The Tuscumbia Society was affiliated with the American Bible Society. It was organized in New York in 1816 and rapidly spread throughout the nation. The Bible Society was interdenominational. The first branch in Alabama was organized in Huntsville in 1820 by Thomas Stringfield, a Methodist circuit rider. Prominent business and professional men were usually the leaders in the local Bible Societies. That was certainly true in Tuscumbia.

These community leaders firmly believed that the Bible and Testament were essential guides "to life eternal." They also believed that it was an excellent guide to daily living. The frontier was rough and often a nasty and brutish place to live. It was thought that studying and following the "Holy Scriptures" would help bring order and civilization to the frontier.

The members believed that most families in the Muscle Shoals frontier already had Bibles and Testaments or could easily afford to buy them. Hence the Society adopted and followed a simple plan. Bibles were sold at cost to those who could afford them and below cost to those less able. A Bible and Testament were given to families living in poverty.

It was not clear how well this program was carried out. Some people felt that the distribution of Bibles and Testaments was totally unnecessary because the Methodist, Presbyterian, and Baptist churches were already a strong presence in the Shoals area. But others felt that the work of these churches did not alter the fact that many families were "destitute of the words of life" as set forth in the Holy Scriptures.

First Presbyterian Church of Tuscumbia Constructed in 1827 (Courtesy of Richard Sheridan)

One of their great successes came among the Chickasaw Indians. Society members felt that there was a great need for Christian literature among the Chickasaws. To meet this need a Bible and Testament was given to each of the Indian students at the Monroe Mission in the Chickasaw nation.

This Mission was established near Corinth, Mississippi in 1822 to educate and Christianize the Indian children in the area. In 1827 the mission had eighty one students. All received a general classroom education. Boys also studied carpentry and farming on a one hundred acre farm while the girls learned spinning and weaving. For religious training a small church size 16 by 16 feet was erected along with a large brush arbor with split long benches and a puncheon floor.

At this period of history before the Indian Removal, the national government and many of the churches were making efforts to educate and Christianize the Indian populations. Some success was enjoyed at the Monroe Mission. Over 150 persons were baptized in this facility.

The members of the Tuscumbia Bible Society learned that numerous families had no Bible hence the task of placing a Bible and Testament in each home was far greater than expected. Their biggest problem seemed to have been a great lack of interest among the public in owning Christian literature. The first annual report of the Bible Society stated that "it is greatly to be lamented that an apathy exists among a large portion of our fellow citizens on this subject."

Perhaps even more surprising was the significant number of people who actually "opposed the circulation of scriptures." There was no organized opposition to the distribution of the Bible and Testament but some individuals spoke out against the project. Apparently the opposition came from people who were encouraged or pressured to buy a Bible but did not wish to do so.

Many people were probably uninterested in owning a Bible and Testament simply because they could neither read nor write. In view of these conditions, the Bible Society strongly recommended to the advocates of the Bible that every possible exertion be used to overcome these obstacles.

The Tuscumbia Society apparently had difficulty getting and keeping a supply of Bibles and Testaments on hand. When the Society was organized, the national headquarters sent seventy five copies as a gift. Shortly thereafter an order of $50 worth of Bibles and Testaments was made. Delivery was slow. Bibles were printed in Louisville, Kentucky and shipped to New Orleans and then reshipped to Tuscumbia by steamboat. Steamboats were just beginning to travel on the Tennessee, Ohio, and Mississippi Rivers. Regular schedules did not exist and service was slow and unreliable.

Despite problems, the Bible Society enjoyed some real success. After one year of operation the Society was in debt and in need of more Bibles and Testaments for distribution. To help solve these problems, members were urged to bring in more donations and dues paying members to support the important work being done.

This new emphasis on reading and studying the Bible and Testament had some long range influence in the established churches. It tended to encourage organized study of the Bible and the growth of Sunday Schools in many churches.

Actually the Bible Society met a real need because buying a Bible was apparently difficult during that time. Mr. T. T. Skillman's bookstore in Tuscumbia advertised several books by name but the Bible was not included. He did have for sale such works as Practical Piety, Letters on Unitarianism, Essays to do Good, and Eastman's Sermons.

One part of the Bible Society report had a very modest ring to it. Society members were reminded of the importance of the work they had undertaken with these words: "The commands of God bind it on us... and sympathy for our perishing fellow men, should ignite our souls and prompt us to every diligence to our power."

Stars Fell on Alabama

The statement "Stars Fell On Alabama" which once helped decorate Alabama car tags, has stimulated much curiosity.

On the night of November 12/13, 1833, most people in the Muscle Shoals area went to bed as usual. A few who went to bed about midnight would have noticed an unusual number of shooting stars streaking across the sky. By three o'clock in the morning the number of meteors or shooting stars had increased to tens of thousands. They entered the earth's atmosphere traveling at about ten miles per second, leaving a long trail of burning material behind.

The light given off by the burning meteors was constant – so much light that many people thought morning had come and the sun was rising. Even the roosters started crowing to meet the dawn. Other livestock thought it was morning. Cows headed for the pasture and chickens left their roosts in search of food.

The people who were awake soon had their families up looking at "the great fireworks display in the sky." One person in Huntsville wrote that everyone was up at three o'clock looking at the "streaming meteors."

The shooting stars seemed to come out of the southwest and traveled in a north-easterly direction. Some seemed to be falling, but so far as it is known, none actually hit the ground.

This great meteor shower covered all the eastern part of the United States from the Gulf of Mexico to Canada. But Alabama seems to have been affected by the display of heavenly fireworks more than other parts of the country. The light from the shooting stars continued until the sun rose and hid the stars with their brightness.

Human reactions to this startling phenomenon were as strange as the event itself. A few people were unimpressed. But many were terrified. Some believed a horrible catastrophe was about to happen. A large number of people thought the world was coming to an end and tried to get right with God. Some knelt and prayed, often confessing sins that startled their earthly hearers. Numerous travelers hurriedly packed their bags and started home to be with their families during the final hours.

The Tennessee Conference of the Methodist Church was meeting in Pulaski, Tennessee at the time. Several dozen ministers were present. Some, especially the younger ministers, believed the meteor shower was announcing the second coming of Jesus. Many conference participants prayed, while others, believing the world was coming to an end, prepared to return to their homes. One of the conference leaders, Dr. Robert Paine, president, teacher and minister at LaGrange College in Franklin County, Alabama, had been born thirty years earlier in the midst of a similar meteor shower. This timely arrival led him to study astronomy. He was thus able to relieve many fears and bring order out of the chaos among the Methodist ministers.

At that time in history, even the best educated men did not really understand what was going on. Newspapers had a field day offering explanations. One theory was that the shooting stars were caused by "sulphureous vapors" exhaled from the bowels of the earth. Another related theory claimed the shooting stars were "combustion of inflammable air, kindled by electricity."

With the coming of the daylight, the shooting stars and the great light they gave off seemed to disappear. Normal conditions existed the following night. But Alabamians certainly had not forgotten the night "Stars Fell on Alabama." The meteor shower was often discussed by Alabamians as late as the 1890's.

There is evidence that the memory continued much longer. In 1934, Carl Cramer wrote a very popular book entitled *Stars Fell on Alabama*, about the people of Alabama and their way of life. A short time later, Mitchell Parish and Frank Perkins wrote and published a ballad with the same title, thus further connecting Alabama with the great meteor shower of 1833.

Meteor showers have been known since ancient times. The shower that appeared over Alabama was a recently formed stream, the Leonids, which reappears every 33 or 34 years, but seldom with the brightness of 1833. The Leonid meteors are associated with their parent comet, Temple-Tuttle.

Women Slave Owners

Before the American Civil War, slavery was a characteristic of life in the Muscle Shoals area. For example, in 1850 the total number of slaves living in Franklin County was 8,197 or about 42 percent of the total county population. The great majority of these slaves lived in what is today Colbert County.

Lauderdale County, with its smaller agricultural area, had only 6,015 slaves. These made up about 35 percent of the total population of the county.

A large portion of the slaves in all Alabama were owned by women. In 1850 Lauderdale County had 535 slave owners. Of this number 77 or 14.4 percent of the total were women. These women in Lauderdale County owned 802 slaves.

The conditions in Franklin County were very much like those of Lauderdale County. There were 545 slave owners in Franklin County. Of this number 55 or about 10 percent were female. These 55 female slave owners owned 596 slaves.

These figures were typical of most of Alabama. In the "hill counties" such as Winston and Marion, where the land did not favor cotton production, there were very few slaves. But in the counties in the Black Belt section of Alabama, the slave population exceeded the white population. For example, in 1850 in Dallas County there were 7,461 white citizens and 22,258 slaves. These slaves were the property of 1284 slave owners of whom 143 were women. These women owned a total of 1,786 slaves, which far exceeded the number owned by women in Franklin and Lauderdale Counties.

Most women slave owners owned only one or two slaves, but some were "big slave owners", which means they owned twenty or more slaves. In Lauderdale County Nancy Pool, Sarah Mary Coffee, and Jane Irion each owned twenty slaves or more. In Franklin County Amanda Barton, Martha Harris, Sarah Fant, Phebe McCulloch, Charlotte Ricks, Mrs. J. M. Winston and Elizabeth Suggs were big slave owners.

These figures seem to indicate that women as well as men had a vested interest in the slave labor system. For this reason as well as many other reasons, women tended to support slavery during the antebellum period in the same way men did.

Women of the Muscle Shoals area became slave owners in three ways. Some received slaves as gifts. Still other women purchased slaves. A majority of the female slave owners received the slaves by inheritance. For example, when Levi Gist died in Franklin County in 1829, his wife and each daughter inherited several slaves.

Available information does not make it clear how the women used the slaves they owned. Apparently, the women who owned several slaves used their labor in the production of cotton much like the men slave owners. But most of the women who owned only one or two slaves, used these slaves as personal servants, workers in boarding houses, seamstresses, etc...

We have no information that would suggest that women and men slave owners treated their slaves any differently. History has generally claimed that women were kind to slaves and generally felt sympathy for the slaves. In the Shoals area there were examples of good and bad female slave owners. One female slave owner was noted, at least by the slaves, for whipping and overworking slaves. On the other hand, Mrs. Levi Gist and her daughter, Sarah, were generally held in high regard by their slaves. The will of Temperance J. Peters provided that $500 should be placed in the hands of her executor for the support and maintenance of an elderly slave.

In many cases a sincere feeling of respect developed between the slaves and their owners. But a slave was a slave and there is no real reason for believing that women treated their slaves better than the men.

Slaves Enjoyed Privileges Not Rights

Some scholars look upon the system of slavery in the United States as being devoid of any human compassion, wherein slaves were treated as animals rather than human beings. Others see the system as one filled with human kindness wherein slaves were well treated by their masters, and were happy and content. The truth is far more complicated than these two extremes suggest.

A look at some religious experiences of the slaves in the Muscle Shoals area may shed some light on this complex aspect of our history.

In the 1840s and 1850s, slaves were welcome in the white churches in the Muscle Shoals area. Many masters encouraged religion among their slaves, and many slaves became members of the established churches. While blacks (slaves and free blacks) were members and often attended worship services, their actual participation and administration of church affairs were strictly in the hands of the whites.

Blacks felt freer and more comfortable in an environment they controlled. In the early 1840s the black members of the Methodist Church established the "African Church" in Florence. Although loosely connected to the Methodist, this church was run by black leaders for blacks and had few if any denominational restrictions. The many regulations governing the slave system made attendance difficult yet large crowds from Florence, and Lauderdale and Franklin (now Colbert) Counties, often gathered at the African Church.

Apparently worship consisted mainly of singing, praying, and preaching, in the early days of the church. These services were held mainly on Sunday afternoons. Gradually prayer meetings began to be held at night. These worship activities were led by "slave ministers" including Dick Kirkman, Cato Hodges, Archie Eggleston, and a slave named William. Two of these men were Baptist and two were Methodist. Hodges and William lived on the Bernard McKiernan plantation in Franklin County, and Kirkman lived in Florence. Eggleston, a Baptist, was probably typical. He preached in a language filled with idioms of the black race but "it spoke to the hearts of the unlearned auditors."

The existence of a slave dominated church in the heart of the slave system was certainly an anomaly. Alabama law did not prohibit slaves preaching but it did require slave ministers to have a license from an established white religious group. The state law also prohibited the assembly of slaves off the plantation for worship and prohibited a slave being off plantation without the master's permission. A strict enforcement of these laws would have closed the African Church. Both state and local laws were largely ignored.

In 1842 white citizens of Florence complained about the noise resulting from the worship and social activities at the African Church. In response to these complaints, the Board of Aldermen ordered the constable "to put a stop to and prohibit the Negroes from holding preaching and other gatherings" within the town limits. This order was repeated numerous times over the years, which suggests that it was never consistently enforced.

As the abolition movement in the United States grew more powerful, whites in the Muscle Shoals area grew increasingly fearful of abolition activities by the slave ministers. In 1848 the aldermen adopted a resolution restricting Negro preaching and prayer meetings in Florence. It stated that no Negro should be allowed to preach except Dick Kirkman and that he was allowed to preach only during the daytime.

The liberated conduct of the slaves seemed to increase in the years just before the Civil War. In 1858 the black members of the Methodist Church received permission from the Florence Aldermen to hold a "fair." Fairs were social and fund raising events common among free Negroes in the North at that time. Apparently the fair in Florence was conducted with great satisfaction because the following year the blacks were authorized to hold another "fair and supper" in the Lauderdale County courthouse. Blacks planned and conducted the entire affair. Food for the supper was contributed, prepared, and served by blacks. According to the Florence Gazette, "The table was supplied with a host of good things... all of which were done up on the nicest style of culinary art." The supper was followed by the fair which consisted of entertainment and the sale of numerous items. Blacks and whites were invited to attend but due to rain only a few white men and no white women attended. The Florence Gazette reported that "the beauty and chivalry of the colored population of Florence were in attendance." The fair and supper produced a net profit of $245.47.

The editor of the Florence Gazette pointed to the supper and fair as evidence that slavery in the South was a kind and humane system. He claimed that the fair and supper proved the abolitionist propaganda was "the big lie."

If slaves had been consulted on this matter, they could have pointed out that the same pages of the Florence Gazette carried advertisements for the buying and selling of human beings as if they were property. They might also have pointed out that slaves enjoyed no constitutionally protected right to worship, assemble, or practice free speech.

Any privilege enjoyed by a slave, could be revoked without recourse at the whim of a discontented master.

Use of Slave Labor by the Town of Florence

The town of Florence was authorized by the Alabama Legislature to organize a town government in 1826, about eight years after the town was created. During these eight years Florence, like other parts of Lauderdale County, was governed locally by the county government.

Florence's first town government was made up of twelve Aldermen elected-at-large annually by the voters of the town. Ordinarily these Aldermen met monthly. The Aldermen chose one of their number to be Mayor. The Mayor presided over aldermanic meetings and performed certain administrative duties. But in practice this official had little more authority than any other Alderman.

Between 1840 and 1861 the town government of Florence experienced essentially the same problems that all towns experience. Street maintenance, pure water, garbage and sewage disposal, fire protection, law and order, and many other less obvious problems commanded attention of the Aldermen. The study of history suggests that these problems have always been matters which cities had to deal with, regardless of time and place. Only the magnitude of the problems and the methods of solution varied over time.

Between 1840 and 1861 Florence had several employees. All except one was part-time and the wages paid were very small. The most important position was the town constable, the only employee paid a set salary for full-time service. Henry Donohoo served as constable for several years and was usually paid between $300 and $500 per year. The county sheriff, then as today, was basically responsible for maintenance of law and order. The constable performed many tasks for the town, but his main duty was law enforcement which aimed at protecting lives and property through his control of slaves and the disorderly element of the population.

Several other Florentines were employed at different times to perform services for the town. Ferdinand Sannoner was employed to prepare a map of Florence. Other men acted as tax assessor and collector and were paid a percentage of the collections. Another official was responsible for maintaining the town clock.

In July 1841 the aldermen established a Rate of Tolls for the Florence wharf and authorized the appointment of a wharf master to supervise wharf activities. According to the ordinance, steamboats, keelboats, flatboats, and rafts were charged set amounts for docking at the Florence docks. For example, the rate for a raft forty feet in length and under was $5.00 per day. Docking fee for a raft between forty and seventy feet was $7.00 and the fee for rafts over seventy feet was $9.00. The toll for a steam boat was $4.00 for the first day and $1.50 per day thereafter for the boats under 200 tons. Six dollars for the first day and $2.00 thereafter was paid for craft over 200 tons.

Robert McCorstin was appointed wharf master in 1841 and held that position for several years. Between July 1841 and February 1843, the wharf master collected $322.50. About twenty five percent of this amount was paid to the wharf master for his services and the balance was used to maintain the docks.

During the 1840s and 1850s the town hired from three to eight slaves each year to work for the town. Slave owners were paid $80 to $150 per year for each adult slave and about $50 for slave boys between the ages of fourteen and eighteen. In 1841, for example, three slaves were hired for $150 each per year, while in 1846 three were hired from among several offers for $80 each. In 1847 five slaves were hired at the rate of $100 each and a slave boy was hired for $40.

Hiring agreements made the town responsible for food, clothing, and lodging. Owners were responsible for medical care and sometimes provided food, clothing, and lodging for the slaves. When the town provided clothing, such items as shoes, blankets, hats, and other factory made items were purchased from local merchants. Garments were made locally. Cloth was purchased by the town and white women were hired to make shirts and pants. For example, in the 1840s Mrs. Mary Field was paid $14 for making clothes. Mrs. Harriet Crowder was paid fifty cents for making one shirt, and Mrs. John Hooks was paid $2.50 for making four pair of pants for slaves.

The town contracted with local townspeople to provide food and lodging for the slaves. In 1845 and 1846 food and lodging cost Florence $40 per slave per year. In 1848 John B. Leftwich provided food and lodging for town slaves at the rate of $50 each per year.

Little can be stated with certainty about the quantity and quality for slave food and lodging. Some comparisons may be helpful. The town on average paid about $3.50 to $4.00 per month for food and lodging for each slave. Students at LaGrange College paid $10 per month for room and board. A local resident of Florence advertised that he would board students attending the Florence Female Academy at the rate of $35 for each five months of term. As these figures suggest, boarding slaves for the town could not have been very profitable. In view of the desire of aldermen to secure this service as cheaply as possible, and the desire of the provider to make as much profit as possible, the quality of food and lodging for the slaves was probably very poor.

Slaves working for the town were usually called "street hands" but their duties were never clearly defined. At various times, they maintained the streets, cleared trees from new streets, dug or filled drainage ditches, built walkways and roads, planted trees, cleared the river banks, repaired the town wells, got water buckets and trash out of the wells, built dikes during floods, removed snow from walkways, cleaned city offices, cut wood, built fires, and did other chores as needed. As this list suggests, slaves did whatever work the town needed done.

Slaves working for the town of Florence must have found some satisfaction in their situation. The slaves had no full-time overseer. Slaves were simply given instruction and sent off to work. They were usually free to set their own pace, take a break at will, and be sociable with persons passing by. Also, after work, slaves were not locked in, but were free to visit about town and socialize with little or no restraint. Hence, living in and working for the town was far better than the more restrictive life on the cotton plantations where most slaves lived and worked.

The forgoing suggests at least two conclusions about Muscle Shoals history. First, the problems of local government in the antebellum period were not greatly different from the problems faced by our modern governments. Second, slavery was not limited to the production of cotton on large plantations, but was a labor system used to advantage in nearly all aspects of Muscle Shoals Life.

Black and White Americans Have Different History

A casual examination of local history clearly reveals that the black and white Americans had some great differences in their history, while being in the same geographical area.

First and perhaps most important, white people never experienced life as a forced laborer. Almost all blacks did. Black slaves were brought into the Shoals area along with the earliest settlers. Their numbers increased with the passage of time. By 1860, the population of Lauderdale County was 17,420 of which 6,781 were black. In 1857 Florence had a special census which revealed that the total population was 1763. This number included 52 slaves and 21 free blacks.

Although blacks and whites lived in the same vicinity, they were generally under different laws. The whites were under the English Common Laws plus acts of the legislature while slaves and free blacks were governed by the Slave Code.

A simple but interesting difference could be seen in some ordinances passed by the Florence Aldermen. An ordinance was passed in the 1830s providing punishment for anyone blocking the streets. This was generally done by leaving wagons and teams of mules or horses standing in the street for long periods of time. Whites found guilty of this misdemeanor paid a fine of $5 to $10. A slave found guilty was punished by thirty nine lashes. In some cases the lash was on the bare back. For other misdemeanors of a similar nature, black women were given twenty lashes.

Punishment by whipping can partially be explained by the fact that slaves could not own property. It is true that slaves sometimes did possess small amounts of money. Sometimes owners permitted their slaves to maintain their own gardens and sell their produce. Also, slaves sometimes worked for other people during their free time to earn money. This was not a common practice. Any money or wealth acquired by a slave could be taken by the slave owner without any court proceedings.

The few free blacks living in the Shoals area were permitted to own, buy and sell property, but were discriminated against in many ways. For example in the city of Florence, the Aldermen imposed a head or poll tax. White males between the ages of twenty one and forty five paid a head tax of $.75 in 1845. This had increased to $2.00 in the 1850s. White women paid no taxes.

The same tax was somewhat different for free blacks. Free black males between the ages of one and fifty paid $3.00 each year after 1854. Free black females also, paid a $3.00 head tax after 1854.

Exceptions were sometimes made. John Rapier Jr., a free black, once requested that the Florence Aldermen reduce his tax from $3.00 to $2.00. The Aldermen agreed to this reduction because of Rapier's "uniform good conduct... and other considerations."

A further examination of the black and white history in the Shoals will reveal many other dissimilarities between black and white people.

Timekeeping in Early Florence

Winnsboro, South Carolina once claimed to have the longest running town clock in the United States. According to local history buffs, this clock has been telling time since 1834...

While Florence, Alabama cannot compete with this claim, it did enjoy the benefits of a town clock for well over a century. The Lauderdale County Courthouse was constructed in 1823. A large dome rested on top of the building. This dome housed a large clock easily visible to the passing public. A bell was attached which could be heard all over town.

In the years before the Civil War these were important instruments in the life of Florentines. Few people owned clocks in their homes and even fewer people had watches. Hence the town clock was the unofficial time piece for the community. The bell announced important events such as the opening of court sessions, calling out the volunteer fire company, the arrival of steamboats or visitors, and other special occasions.

During December of most years, a committee of three Aldermen was appointed to contract with a capable person to "keep the town clock clean and in good working order." This clock keeper was expected to wind up the clock and make adjustments and repairs as needed.

Henry Donohoo agreed to keep the town clock during 1840 for $50.00. He also served as the town constable for which he was paid $100 per annum. The amount paid for keeping the town clock appear to be a paltry sum but there was competition for this job. In 1843 the town contracted with Mr. Charles White to keep the town clock for one year for a mere $25.00. However it was stipulated that if it needed cleaning during the year, he would be paid an additional $15.00. The Aldermen quickly learned that frugality had a price.

After a few weeks, some of the more alert citizens noticed that while the clock worked fine, the bell had ceased to ring. An investigating committee quickly discovered that the bell had been immobilized by White. He explained that the vibrations resulting from the ringing of the bell interfered with the clock so that it would not keep proper time. Hence to avoid constantly resetting the clock, he had simply disconnected the bell. The Aldermen took a firm stand. It was ordered that the bell must be rung on all appropriate occasions. Apparently neither the Aldermen nor Mr. White were happy but he did continue caring for the clock.

In 1845 Henry Donohoo again offered to take charge of the town clock for $50 per annum but he was under bid by Mr. William Allen, who offered to take the job for forty five dollars. Allen was given the contract but only after he entered into bond for the faithful performance of the assigned duty. In 1848, Mr. Z. P. Morrison agreed to clean the clock once a year and keep it in good order for forty dollars.

For 1849, Julius House was elected to serve as town constable and "clock winder" for $300. This arrangement must have been unsatisfactory because after two months Henry Donohoo was again given the job. He was expected to keep the clock "clean and… in good order for the remainder of the year for $40." Donohoo continued rendering this service until 1855 after which several men including John A. Portlock, S. S. Cutler, and N. H. Rice served as clock keeper at various times.

By 1860, citizens of Florence were complaining about the clock. The Aldermen reacted by employing James McPeters at $50 per year but with the stipulation that there would be no pay unless the clock was kept in good order. McPeters' service must have been satisfactory because his contract was renewed for 1861. The care for the town clock was almost certainly discontinued when the Union soldiers arrived in Florence in April 1862.

During this time period from 1840 to 1861, clocks and/or watches constituted real wealth and were therefore subject to a tax along with other property. In the 1840s the city tax on a brass clock was $1.00 per year while the owner of a wooden clock paid $.50. The owner of a gold watch paid $1.00 per year while the owner of a silver watch paid $.50 cents. This tax continued basically unchanged until after the Civil War except the tax on clocks was shifted from their material composition to the value of the clock. By 1860 the owner of a clock valued at $20 or more paid $1.00 per year while a clock valued at less than $20 was taxed at fifty cents.

The erecting of a town clock for public use started in the 14th century Italian town squares. The practice spread over Europe and North America and continued well into the early twentieth century when clocks and watches began to be produced in mass quantity and sold at low cost.

Railroading in the Muscle Shoals Area

The Muscle Shoals in the Tennessee River was a problem which almost cried out for solution. In the late 1700s, settlers realized that the Muscle Shoals in the Tennessee River was an obstacle to river travel. Nothing was done about the problem until 1830, when the state government with federal funding started building a canal around the Shoals. But money and technical "know-how" were inadequate to the task. Hence the first canal project turned out to be a failure.

Also in 1830, another project aimed at solving the problem caused by the Muscle Shoals was launched. The first railroad in the United States was started in Maryland in 1828. On hearing of this new "mechanical device", David Hubbard, a businessman in Tuscumbia, travelled to Baltimore to see how the railroad actually worked. He returned home determined to launch a railroad project in Alabama.

In January 1830 the State Legislature chartered the Tuscumbia Railroad. The railroad, the first west of the Appalachian Mountains, ran two miles from Tuscumbia to the Tennessee River. Rails were made of wood but were soon strengthened by nailing a thin iron strip along the top of the wood rail. Over these rails the cars were pulled by mules and horses.

A short time later the Alabama Legislature chartered the Tuscumbia, Courtland, and Decatur Railroad. Construction began immediately in Tuscumbia. By 1833 the railroad extended eastward beyond Leighton. The forty-two mile track was completed through Courtland to Decatur in November 1836.

The investors in the T. C. and D. RR expected that steamboats would bring freight up river to the Tuscumbia Landing, where it would be placed on railroad cars and sent to Decatur. There it would be placed on another steamboat and sent on upriver. The investors in the railroad were in effect gambling that the canal around the Shoals would fail and that the new method of transportation would succeed. They were also aware that cotton planters needed a dependable way to get their bales of cotton to a riverboat landing for shipping to New Orleans.

The T. C. and D. RR not only opened a new form of transportation to the Shoals, it introduced some new technology. A four-wheeled steam engine, known as the "Comet" was completed in 1835. It was built for the T. C. and D. RR by the West Point Foundry in New York City. The foundry had built the first steam locomotive in America in 1830. This engine was known as the "Best Friend" and was put into operation in South Carolina.

The Comet included one major new innovation. In the early days of railroading, the frame which functioned to hold the various parts of the locomotive together was made of wood. Trains were lightweight and operated at slow speeds. Under these conditions wood frames were usually acceptable. The Comet was unique in that its frame was made entirely of iron bars securely bolted together. While wood frames remained common for the next 20 years, the iron frame gradually became the standard.

In 1835, shortly after the Comet was placed in service, problems began to occur. The Comet simply did not have the power to pull cars loaded with freight and passengers. Hence the mules were brought back to pull the passenger cars.

The Comet had trouble starting and stopping when the track was wet or oily. Due to limited traction, the driving wheel would simply spin. To solve this problem, the T. C. and D. RR installed sandboxes on the locomotive in 1836. This apparently was the earliest known use of sand to increase traction. Sandboxes were placed in front of the drive wheels. The engineer was able to discharge the contents of the boxes onto the rails as needed. The sandbox method of increasing traction became a common practice in the 1840s.

While these innovations may not have impressed the ordinary traveler, there existed near Decatur another practical innovation which would certainly have commanded respect. A passenger arriving in Decatur and wanting to cross the Tennessee River would head for the ferry. There he would find a boat attached securely to one end of a 900 yard rope. The other end of the rope was attached to a large tree about 900 yards up river. The rope was kept out of the water by nine buoys. The ferryboat was propelled back and forth across the river by water power. By inclining the head of the boat to the right or the left, the pressure of the current against a broad plank fixed below the sides of the boat carried it from one back to another.

Our ancestors did not have the sophisticated machinery and power sources available today, but they did have a practical understanding of the world they lived in and could use the resources available to them to great advantage.

National Highway Proposed for Florence

Transportation has always been a major factor in the economic development of the Muscle Shoals area. In the very early days, the Tennessee River and Indian trails were the main means of travel and transportation. As settlers moved into the area they built crude roads such as the Natchez Trace, the Byler Road, and the Jackson Military Road. While these improvements were important, they left much to be desired.

In the late 1820s a glimmering of hope for a national highway surfaced. In 1827 the Secretary of War ordered the Army Corp of Engineers to plan a national highway from Zanesville, Ohio to Florence, Alabama. According to the directive, the road was to proceed southward from Zanesville through Maysville and Lexington, Kentucky and Nashville, Tennessee, to Florence, Alabama.

The study for this highway was completed in July, 1828. It included a careful examination of several possible routes the proposed highway might take. It also studied the problems that would have to be dealt with in actual construction.

This proposed Zanesville-Florence highway was intended to be a southern branch of the famous National Road that started in Cumberland, Maryland and was gradually built westward through Zanesville, Ohio to St. Louis. For many years this road was considered the best constructed and most popular highway in America. Part of the highway is still in use today.

The roads already existing along the proposed Zanesville-Florence highway route were carefully studied also. Most of these roads covered only short distances and were designed to meet the needs of local communities rather than the states and the nation. They were poorly constructed. Low wet lands were generally avoided in order to have firm foundations for the road bed and to avoid expensive causeways. Also, existing roads generally crossed streams at fordable points thereby avoiding costs of bridges.

Existing roads from Nashville southward to Florence generally followed what is today US Highway 43. Much of the route was once an Indian trail. This trail was used by many of the early settlers coming into the area. In 1817-20 the builders of the Jackson Military road generally followed the Indian trail and then ten years later in 1827 the National Road survey followed the Jackson Highway from Nashville to Florence.

But there was one exception in Alabama. The proposed national highway was planned to cross the Shoals Creek about three miles eastward and below the point of the Military Road crossing.

The plans for the Zanesville-Florence highway called for an eighty foot clearing through the forest. Within this cleared area was a thirty foot grubbing lane in which all roots were removed. Then within this grubbing lane, a twenty foot wide highway would be constructed. The highway would have a nine inch deep clay road bed covered with six inches of gravel and limestone. This macadamized road was the best form of highway construction known in America at the time.

The Zanesville-Florence highway would be approximately 708.5 miles in length. The estimated total cost was set at $4,200,309 or $5928.45 per mile average.

Advantages of good roads over bad or no roads were obvious. Travel was faster, safer, and much more comfortable. It was estimated that a businessman shipping goods over the proposed highway would pay $1.35 per 100 lb for each hundred miles. This was far less than typical shipping rates at the time.

Very few people in Congress or on the frontier spoke out against the Zanesville-Florence highway. But it was not to be. The proposal was killed by one of the greatest friends of the Muscle Shoals area, Andrew Jackson.

No bill was introduced to Congress authorizing the construction of the entire highway. Supporters planned to build the highway in pieces. The Maysville Road Bill was passed by Congress authorizing the construction of a part of the highway from Maysville to Lexington, Kentucky. When this bill arrived of the desk of President Andrew Jackson in 1831 he immediately vetoed it. Considering Jackson's great interest in Tennessee and North Alabama, many of his friends in Nashville and Florence were surprised by the veto.

The people who were surprised did not really know Andrew Jackson. He was a firm believer that highway construction and other such improvements entirely within a state, should be paid for by the State rather than the national government.

Also, politics was influential in his thinking. The Maysville Road Bill called for construction of a highway in the home state and near the home of Henry Clay, one of Jackson's strongest political opponents. At that period of time both men were interested in the upcoming presidential election. Jackson was never a man to give an advantage to an opponent, especially one he did not like.

The veto was very unfortunate for Florence and all of northwest Alabama. The construction of the Zanesville-Florence highway would have given a major boost to the developing economy in Northwest Alabama.

Florence Was Not Always a Quiet and Peaceful Town during the Holiday Season

In the 1850s the Florence Aldermen enacted an ordinance imposing a 10 p.m. curfew during the Christmas/New Year holiday season. The same ordinance was operative year after year. The purpose of the curfew was to clear the streets of troublemakers so that decent folk could sleep in peace and security.

At that time the population of Florence was 897 whites, 526 slaves, and 21 free blacks. Very few of these people owned or had access to watches or clocks. To make everyone aware of the curfew, the town constable was required to ring the large metal bell on top of the Masonic Building at 10 p.m. every night during the holiday season.

Curfew, bell ringing, and other such ordinances, required enforcement. Normally Florence had one constable elected annually by the qualified voters in the city. An election was held in 1859, when Mr. Edward Brown, with 69 popular votes, was elected constable over two competitors. He was also appointed sexton and city tax collector, which brought his total salary to $300 per year.

The maintenance of law and order during the holiday season was beyond the ability of one man. The Aldermen sometimes employed an "assistant constable" to work from about December 20 to January 2 each year. The constable seldom worked at night. The assistant usually worked the streets at night and was paid $1.50 per day. The Aldermen also employed four or more persons each year to help maintain law and order and protect property. These individuals were given various titles such as patrolmen, watchmen, and policemen. At night they patrolled the streets and alleys checking on buildings, looking for fires, herding drunks home or to jail, and quieting the noisy elements of society. They normally did not have the power to make arrests, and their only means of enforcing the law was by diplomacy or physical strength. These workers were paid $1.00 to $1.50 per night.

The build-up of law enforcement suggests that the holiday season was a time for criminality rather than celebration, fun, good cheer, and fellowship toward all men.

Slaves usually benefited from "the holiday spirit." There was usually little work to be done in the fields during the holiday season, hence slaves had more free time than usual. Some slave masters like Bernard McKiernan in Franklin County, let their slaves produce garden products and sell them in Tuscumbia and Florence during the year. Also, some slaves were given small amounts of money before Christmas. Slaves thus often had money with which to buy the means of enjoying and celebrating the holidays. Also, rural slaves were often permitted to come into town when free from labor. They joined with urban slaves in celebrating without the usual restraints. Doing business with slaves without the owner's permission was illegal but selling whiskey was a common practice. Fights, loud noise, and other more serious criminal activity was typical of the holiday season.

The holiday season was a time when normal restraints on free and non-free people were relaxed. Individuals were freer than usual to celebrate in their own way.

Christmas and Politics in 1860

The Christmas season in 1860 was an exciting and disturbing time in the Muscle Shoals area. The excitement came not from rampant commercialism or the thrill of giving and receiving gifts.

Much of the excitement during the 1860 Christmas season grew out of political activity. Voters were called upon to make one of the most important political decisions in the history of Alabama. The question was, "Should Alabama secede from the Union?"

In early 1860 the Alabama legislature feared that a "Black Republican" would be elected president to the United States. This fear led the legislature to pass a resolution directing Governor A. B. Moore to arrange for a statewide election to select delegates to a convention if Abraham Lincoln was elected President. The plan was for these delegates to meet in Montgomery and decide if Alabama would secede from the Union.

Abraham Lincoln was elected President, and Governor Moore ordered the election of delegates to be held on Christmas Eve, December 24th. Franklin and Lauderdale Counties were ordered to elect two delegates from each county.

Political campaigning began almost immediately after the election date was set. Numerous public meetings were held in both counties. Speakers appealed to the voters' passions and fears. The loudest and most vocal campaigners favored immediate secession, while many others gave their support to candidates who favored a more cautious policy. One voter attended a meeting in Tuscumbia and came away feeling that a "good many here are for disunion, probably a majority."

On Christmas Eve 1860, voters went to the polls and cast their vote. John A. Steel and R. S. Watkins were elected in Franklin County; Sydney C. Posey and Henry C. Jones were elected from Lauderdale County. All were opposed to immediate secession.

While politics seemed to dominate the public thought, the spirit of Christmas and especially the practice of gift giving went on. The experiences of Joshua Burns Moore and his wife were probably typical.

Moore, a self-educated lawyer, had established a very successful law practice in Franklin County. In 1858 he had married eighteen-year-old Ella Pearsal. They lived near the Pearsal plantation a few miles from South Florence and Tuscumbia.

December 24th was Ella's twentieth birthday. She, as women have been known to do, let her husband know that she expected two gifts from him, one for her birthday and another gift for Christmas.

On Christmas Eve, Moore hitched his horse to his buggy and traveled to Tuscumbia. After voting, he purchased several "Christmas treats" and returned home. That Christmas night after his wife was sound asleep and Santa Claus was busy travelling the world over, Moore placed a $75 diamond ring in Ella's stocking which had been carefully hung by the fireplace. She discovered the gift early Christmas morning. Moore noted in his diary that she seemed surprised and delighted.

Ella had a surprise for her husband in the form of a new shirt. In that era, shirts were not mass produced and mass marketed, but they could be acquired from a seamstress or produced by slave labor. But Moore carefully and appreciatively noted in his diary that Ella had made this shirt with her own hands.

The Moore family ended their Christmas activities by eating Christmas dinner to which several close relatives and friends had been invited.

Part Three: The Civil War in the Muscle Shoals Area

Fort Sumter Changed Life in the Shoals

Historical events often have consequences far beyond the abilities of man to foresee and appreciate. The bombardment of Fort Sumter in the port of Charleston, South Carolina, by the Confederate military on April 12, 1861, was one such event.

This military action signified the beginning of the Civil War. The people of the Shoals in 1861 eagerly sought information about what was going on in the country. The newspaper offices, the post offices, and especially the telegraph offices were besieged by seekers of the latest information.

Telegraph offices were located in Tuscumbia, South Florence, and Florence. This was the principal and most current source of information, but the weekly newspapers remained the most complete source of news.

Travelers and workers on the Memphis and Charleston Railroad were eagerly sought out for information about activities in other parts of the South.

When Alabama seceded from the Union, many people believed there would be no war. After the war actually began, military companies were more rapidly organized and offered for service in the Confederate military. The companies were given such names as the University Grays, College Grays, Florence Guards, Lauderdale Rifles, Silver Grays (old men) and others. Companies organized later in the war were not usually given specific names other than the military designation such as Company A or B, etc...

On April 27, 1861, a great public meeting was held on the campus of the Florence Wesleyan University to celebrate the departure of the "University Grays." Rev. William H. Mitchell, pastor of the First Presbyterian Church, gave a rousing speech entitled "Lauderdale Volunteers." After several other celebratory activities, each soldier was given a Bible. The unit departed at 2 p.m. for Richmond, Virginia, where the University Grays became Company H in the 4th Alabama Infantry Regiment.

It was common knowledge that students and faculty at the University of LaGrange and Military Academy were eager to go on active duty. Within a few months these institutions were closed, and many of the patriotic young men had given their lives and limbs to an insatiable appetite of war.

Many could not join fully in the excitement. One mother who knew that her son would soon be entering the military and felt the impending loss, wrote "It is certainly a very solemn time among the people."

War not only rearranged and destroyed human life, it changed the economic conditions within the community. Following the bombardment of Fort Sumter, there was a need for almost every kind of military material. The Muscle Shoals was not an industrial area, but there was a demand for all that the factories could produce, and that was especially true for the cloth used in making uniforms.

A local company, Milner, Wood, Wrenn, and Company, had produced over 117,000 yards of cloth in 1860 in its Cowpen Creek factory. Yet the demand for cloth was such that it tried to buy and produce more. In May 3, 1861, this company wrote to a business in Panola, Mississippi, offering to buy 700 or 800 yards of gray jean material. The buyers gave assurance that the money would be ready at any time the goods could be had. Similar letters were received as industries all over the South scrambled to meet the rapidly emerging military needs.

The cannons that blasted Fort Sumter in April 1861 set in motion forces that changed a whole way of life in the Muscle Shoals Area.

Florence Bridge Destroyed During the Civil War

One of the biggest losses to the Muscle Shoals area during the Civil War came at the hands of the Confederate army.

About one month after the fall of Forts Henry and Donelson in February, 1862, a Confederate army commanded by General Albert Sidney Johnston was retreating southward through Tennessee and Northern Alabama to the Corinth, Mississippi area. The Yankees were following closely behind. On March 18, 1862, Confederate General Johnston ordered Colonel B. H. Helm, then in Tuscumbia, to make silent preparations to burn the Florence Bridge as soon as the enemy gunboats passes Eastport or the enemy approached Florence from the north side of the river. The order was intended to slow the advancing Union army.

On April 13th, Union General O. M. Mitchel, after having occupied Huntsville and Decatur, reported that his troops were advancing cautiously upon Tuscumbia and Florence.

Col. Helm carried out his orders. The Florence Bridge was burned. The citizens of the Muscle Shoals area were once again left without a bridge to connect the two sides of the river.

The destruction of the bridge was a great loss to the civilian population but provided little benefit for the Confederate military. The Union army quickly crossed the Tennessee River and was well established on the north and south side of the Tennessee River. The bridge burning had little if any influence in slowing the advance of the federal troops.

The Florence Bridge at that time was owned by the Memphis and Charleston Railroad. It had two levels. The lower deck was a one-lane toll bridge over which pedestrians, wagons and other such traffic could move. The upper deck was a railroad bridge on the spur line extending to Florence from Tuscumbia.

Florentines valued the bridge highly. Before the Union army arrived in the Tennessee Valley, two Union gunboats came up the river to Florence. At that time a group of Florentines met with the squadron commander and requested that the Florence Bridge not be destroyed. The commander believed the bridge had no military significance. He assured the Florentines that the gunboats would not destroy the bridge.

Actually the civilians themselves were highly destructive. When the Union gunboats first appeared, three steamers partially loaded with Confederate military supplies were tied up at the Florence Docks. To prevent capture by the Yankees, some civilians hastily set the steamers on fire. All three were destroyed although the Yankees arrived in time to salvage some of the supplies.

Ferry Used in Crossing Major Rivers

For the remaining war years and five years thereafter, a ferry operated irregularly between Florence and South Florence. In 1870 the bridge was rebuilt on its original foundation.

The Arrest of Rev. William H. Mitchell

About thirteen months after the Civil War began at Fort Sumter, South Carolina, Union soldiers marched into and occupied the Muscle Shoals area. The 10th Kentucky Regiment, commanded by twenty-nine-year-old Colonel John Marshall Harlan, occupied Florence.

While no local government office was abolished by the occupying army, for all practical purposes, local government ceased to exist in the presence of an overwhelming enemy military force. Also, the freedoms guaranteed by the Bill of Rights were no longer protected.

It was not the announced purpose of the Union Army to interfere with normal local business and political activities, but that is what happened. Some businesses closed. Schools, the university, and churches in the occupied area either closed or proceeded with an irregular and an unpredictable schedule. These changes usually occurred without clash or conflict, but one event stands out as the exception.

The official policies of the Presbyterian Church called for their ministers to pray during worship services for an established government and its leaders. Rev. William H. Mitchell, pastor of the First Presbyterian Church in Florence and a loyal Confederate supporter, soon found himself in trouble. On several occasions Union soldiers attended his Sunday morning worship services without any disturbance. On Sunday morning, July 27, 1862, Rev. Mitchell prayed as usual for President Jefferson Davis, his cabinet, the Confederate Congress, and for the success of the Confederate Armies.

Union Colonel Harlan was present during this worship service. After the prayer was completed, Colonel Harlan arose from his seat, walked to the front of the church, and ordered the worship service to cease. Rev. Mitchell was arrested. Apparently no specific charges were mentioned and no arrest warrant was served. Mitchell was carried to the district headquarters of the Union Army in Tuscumbia.

Under more settled peacetime conditions, this action by Colonel Harlan would have aroused several constitutional questions, but in wartime conditions, little if any attention was given to the obvious breach of first amendment rights. The people of Florence were "greatly excited" about the arrest of Rev. Mitchell. But they and the Confederate military could do nothing when the United States army failed to use its power to protect their freedom of worship.

After a few days as a prisoner of the Union military in Tuscumbia, Rev. Mitchell was sent to a prison in Alton, Illinois. No one seems to know exactly what happened to him during the next few months. But apparently some influential friends intervened on his behalf with Union authorities. In October 1862 he returned to Florence and resumed his ministerial duties and his service as President of the Florence Female Synodical College without further interference from the Union military. It is not clear whether or not he continued to publicly pray for the Confederacy.

For the remainder of the Civil War and some years afterwards, Rev. Mitchell continued his ministerial duties and his service with the Florence Female Synodical College. He resigned from the church pastorate in 1871. The following year he resigned from the Synodical College. Rev. Mitchell died on October 2, 1872.

In a sense this ends the story of Rev. Mitchell's arrest by Colonel John Harlan. But there is another chapter.

After the Civil War, Colonel Harlan returned to Kentucky and established a successful law practice. He was elected attorney general of his state. In 1877, he was appointed Associate Justice of the U. S. Supreme Court. He served in this position for approximately thirty-four years, during which time he made a great reputation fighting for the human rights guaranteed under the U. S. Constitution.

Judge Harlan's decisions were usually aimed at broadening and protecting the civil rights of African-Americans. In this regard Judge Harlan continued to greatly excite the people of Florence and the citizens of Alabama.

Shoals Women in the Civil War

In January 1861 the Muscle Shoals area was occupied by a divided people. Delegates from all parts of Alabama were in Montgomery debating whether Alabama should secede from the Union or not. Franklin and Lauderdale Counties had elected delegates who opposed secession. While these delegates probably represented the majority of the people in northwest Alabama, they did not reflect the thinking of a vocal group of women.

At that time women could not vote or hold public office but they made their voices heard. Just before secession actually occurred, a group of Tuscumbia women "acting independently" formed an association and immediately adopted a resolution agreeing not to buy anything made north of the Mason and Dixon Line after January 16, 1861. The women believed it was their duty to comfort and help their husbands, brothers, and young men to the utmost in case of war.

Similar sentiments were expressed elsewhere. In Florence a group of southern sympathizers suggested the passage of a local military tax. A pro-Union group quickly spoke out strongly against the proposed tax. A group of women in Eufaula was so angered by this pro-Union attitude they volunteered to pay the tax. To add further insult, they voted to send a hoop skirt to the chairman of the pro-Union group as a mark of his cowardice.

Women in the Muscle Shoals area showed their southern sympathies by making flags, urging patriotic activities among relatives and friends, and participating in and speaking out at public rallies. While attending a "Great War Meeting" in Florence one lady became so excited by the plea for recruits that she stood up and offered her dozen sons for military service as soon as they became large enough to bear arms.

The women of the Shoals were not superficial patriots. In June 1861 the pastor of the Florence Presbyterian Church, Rev. William H. Mitchell, abandoned his text for the Sunday morning sermon and started urging the women to organize a society to make bandages and other such items for the Confederate hospitals. The Manse was offered as a meeting place where this work could be carried on. That afternoon swarms of ladies of all ages appeared for work. Mrs. John Coffee gave instruction in rolling bandages. The minister reported that it was incredible to see how much was done in a few hours by fair hands and patriotic hearts. This kind of work became increasingly organized. Sewing circles, military aid societies, and other such organizations came into existence in many communities and contributed their bit to the war effort.

The battles of Fort Henry and Fort Donelson in February 1862 further escalated the involvement of women in the war effort. After these battles, many Confederate soldiers were brought to Florence and Tuscumbia for reuperation and rest. Homes were opened and empty buildings were hastily made into local hospitals. The patriotic ladies now worked with the realities of war.

In April 1862 thundering guns announced the beginning of the Battle of Shiloh. Realizing that hundreds of wounded men would soon be moved from the battlefield to the surrounding communities, the Florence Military Aid Society under the leadership of President Mary Dyas prepared for action. Mrs. Dyas and some of her colleagues drove a wagon to Iuka, Mississippi. From that point wounded men were brought to Florence and placed in private homes and the local medical centers. Other local ladies assembled at the boat landings in Tuscumbia and Florence with vehicles of every kind and carried wounded men from incoming steamboats to local hospitals and private homes for the best medical care available under the circumstances.

Actually the service rendered by women during the Battle of Shiloh, was probably their finest hour during the Civil War. Shortly after Shiloh, the Union military occupied the Tennessee Valley. Much of the organized support of the Confederacy was no longer possible. Open advocacy of Southern patriotism had to be restrained.

But indications of their southern sympathies were clearly evident throughout the war. Several dances were held for Confederate soldiers and officers. On one occasion in 1864 the young ladies of Florence gave a "mixed dance" for Confederate officers and enlisted men. One of the privates wrote that he had "supreme pleasure" of giving a high-ranking officer a "pretty rough push" when the officer stepped on his partner's dress. A Confederate lieutenant from New Orleans was impressed with the North Alabama women. He wrote that the Alabama women were "more patriotic, prettier, and used less snuff than [women] in certain portions of North Georgia."

While the Confederate sympathizers watched and acted with caution as the "nightmare of war" stretched on year after year, they did not watch in silence. After Mrs. E. A. O'Neal's home was fired upon by the Union army and later entered by a drunken soldier demanding whiskey, she wrote her husband "I hope [I] never see a YANKEE again. [It is] a horrible name to me." When Florence was occupied by the Union Army in 1862, one young woman used such invectives as "vandals," "barbarians," "Yankee hirelings," "Northern marauders," and "shameless outlaws," in a letter describing the soldiers. These feminine attitudes continued with little change throughout the remainder of the Civil War.

Salt: A Major Problem for People in Wartime

While driving through the western part of Virginia, the reader may be greeted with a sign which states, "WELCOME TO SALTVILLE, SALT CAPITAL OF THE CONFEDERACY." Many of us have never heard of Saltville; and the use of salt is not a major concern to most of us today. Such has not always been true. The early settlers in the Tennessee Valley had difficulty getting salt. No significant salt deposits exist in North Alabama. In the early 1800s much of the salt brought into the Valley came from Saltville, Virginia. It was produced, placed in sacks or barrels, and shipped down the Tennessee River on flatboats.

In the 1820s when the steamboats started traveling up and down the River, salt was easily brought in from other parts of the country and from Europe. While salt was essential to the way of life developing in Alabama, it ceased to be a matter of concern as the supply became adequate and dependable.

The Civil War brought salt back to the forefront of human problems. Both Union and Confederate leaders realized that salt was a necessary element in the life of a well-fed army.

Salt served many purposes in the Tennessee Valley. It added taste to food and contributed to good health for humans and animals. Large quantities were used in the tanning process during which animal hides were made into useable leather. Even larger quantities were used in preserving foods such as cheese, butter, fish, and meats.

The first "killing frost" each fall brought on "hog killing" time. Animals were slaughtered, cut up, and the yearly supply of meat preserved with the application of large quantities of salt to the meat. The meat was then stored in various ways in the smokehouses of that era. Canning and refrigeration were unknown at the time; salt had to be used to prevent spoilage. Thus, if the salt supply was inadequate, the food supply was inadequate for the soldiers and for the people on the home front.

From the beginning of the Civil War, Union leaders adopted a policy aimed at cutting off the supply of salt to the Confederacy. Military raids were conducted by the Union army and navy against "salt works" along the coast where salt was being extracted from sea water. Raids by the Union cavalry against inland salt works greatly reduced production. The Union blockade prevented foreign imports, and control over the rivers and railroads cut off most internal shipments of salt and other products. Shortages of barrels, sacks, kettles, and other equipment necessary to the salt industry added more problems.

Within one year after the Civil War started, salt was in very short supply in the Confederacy. In some sections such as the Tennessee Valley of North Alabama, there was simply no salt to be had.

Of all the shortages people experienced during the Civil War, the lack of salt probably commanded the greatest amount of attention. People naturally tried to find substitutes. Saltpeter was sometimes used but it was in very short supply and was needed for making ammunition. Barrels, sacks, and other items which had once contained salt, even the floor of smokehouses, were boiled to secure salt brine. Ashes, especially from corncobs, were used as a substitute. One wartime recipe for bread and cakes suggested that women use one part ashes mixed with two parts of sour milk, as a substitute for salt. Some people gave up the practice of slaughtering their annual meat supply in the fall. They chose instead to slaughter an animal every four or five weeks as needed, thus eliminating the problem of preserving large quantities of meat. In other cases, meat was cooked and then packed in barrels of lard. While this method could preserve some meats, it was not a satisfactory substitute for salt. Other experiments were tried, usually to little avail.

Political leaders in Alabama recognized this salt problem shortly after the Civil War began and tried to deal with it. As shortages grew, merchants began hoarding salt and increasing prices. Governor A. B. Moore denounced this "unpatriotic and wicked" practice of charging citizens unreasonably high prices. The denunciation of hoarding and price gouging continued throughout the war. Early in the war, the governor was authorized by the legislature to seize for public use salt secretly stored or held for high price. This law was difficult to enforce and had little impact.

To increase the supply of salt, the state owned lands in Clark and Washington Counties which contained salt deposits were opened for private development. Unfortunately, the quantity of salt produced here was limited and the quality very poor. The State signed several contracts with salt merchants for the purchase of salt when available. State agents were stationed at various salt works with authority to buy salt. Private citizens and businesses set up "salt works" on the coast where salt was extracted from sea water. These operations were small, difficult to manage, and constantly exposed to Union attack.

Some State officials took actions specifically to help North Alabama. Saltville, Virginia, where 10,000 bushels of salt were often produced each day, was looked upon as the main supplier for North Alabama. Unfortunately this was never a stable source. From February 1862 through the remainder of the war, the Union military controlled the Tennessee River and railroads most of the time, thereby restricting the distribution of Virginia salt in North Alabama.

Despite all these efforts, the quality of life in the Tennessee Valley was seriously hurt as a result of the shortage of salt during the Civil War.

South Florence during Wartime

The Civil War disrupted normal life in South Florence, but some businesses and other activities did continue.

The people in South Florence, also known as Southport, were not outspoken supporters of secession, but they did support the Confederate cause. In May 1861, about a month after the Civil War started in Charleston, South Carolina, a cavalry company was organized in South Florence. Officers were elected under the direction of Joshua Burns Moore and other local leaders.

Normal life was further disrupted in early 1862 when Union military forces began pushing into the Shoals area. In April of that year, a Confederate regiment commanded by Colonel B. F. Helm burned the railroad bridge to keep it from falling into the hands of federal troops. Soon thereafter the railroads and the Tennessee River were controlled by the Union military. As a result, most travel and shipping were discontinued.

Some business did go on in South Florence. Walker's Store and Price and Simpson's Mercantile Company both of which had operated since 1841 were destroyed by Union soldiers in the early part of the war. At least one and probably more businesses continued to operate. While nearly all shipping on the Tennessee River eventually disappeared, some of the cotton trade continued at least in the earlier part of the war. One planter sold 52 bales of cotton with the expectation that it would be shipped down river from South Florence in late 1861.

Nearly all consumer goods were in short supply during the war. People eagerly sought the opportunity to buy what they needed. In the closing months of the war, a river boat loaded with articles generally sold by retail merchants came into the area. This boat/store, operated by a Captain Danley, came to South Florence for a few days on several different occasions. Customers were welcomed aboard. Apparently business was very good. One planter went to South Florence twice to do some shopping on the boat/store but changed his mind on both occasions when he saw the large crowd of "negroes, women, boys, and men" on the boat. This boat/store was comparable to the "Rolling Store" which became popular in rural areas of Alabama in the 1920's and 1930's.

Much military activity occurred in the South Florence area, although no major battles were fought there. South Florence was a good place for crossing the river or for landing riverboats. In 1862 federal troops occupied the area for several months. For the remainder of the war, either Confederate or Federal troops were there much of the time.

Union Transport Boats

Some of the soldiers stayed in a boarding house run by a "Mrs. P." Both armies used South Florence as a crossing point and a recreation area. On one occasion the local residents were surprised to see a large number of federal soldiers bathing in the river. One of the observers enjoyed watching the bathers through a "spy glass."

Military men sometimes erected a pontoon bridge to cross the river while civilians found the crossing to be a real problem. With the ferry out of business and the railroad bridge burned, the only way for a civilian to cross the river was to hire a skiff and a rower. This crossing cost at least fifty cents and was very uncertain. Skiffs and rowers often could not be found.

During the Civil War, South Florence was an information center for people in the area. With the riverboats and trains out of service most of the time, many people in the area traveled to South Florence to get the latest telegraphic news. Unfortunately this source of information was not at all dependable. In the early part of the war the Confederate government took over the telegraph system. During much of the time, the system was out of order, and when working, it served mainly Confederate military needs. Apparently the statement "no news by telegraph" became a common saying in the area. People eagerly purchased newspapers, even newspapers three or four months old when they could be found. Mail service was completely cut off. Letters and other written communication were delivered by friends and relatives when possible.

When the Civil War ended, South Florence had very little to look forward to. The riverboats were soon back in operation, doing business mainly at the Tuscumbia Landing and the Florence Port. The Memphis and Charleston Railroad was back in operation by the end of 1865, but service on the spur line to Florence was not resumed until 1870 when the railroad bridge was rebuilt and reopened.

In the postwar years South Florence did not thrive. It simply had no reason for being. Tuscumbia and Florence were far more accessible, and more able to meet the business needs of people in northwest Alabama.

South Florence was never chartered by the State Legislature and therefore had no town government. Several warehouses were located there along with retail businesses, a boarding house, and a railroad station after a railroad was built to Florence. Dr. William H. Harrington, chair of chemistry at LaGrange College, was a physician and surgeon. He maintained a medical practice in South Florence in the 1820's. Some lawyers came to the community when their services were needed but apparently never maintained offices there. There is little or no indication that industrial, religious, or educational institutions existed there. South Florence was a small community with a good natural port but never a thriving, growing community.

South Florence was a river port from the beginning until all business and community activities gradually died out or moved elsewhere. By the late 19th or early 20th century, mother nature had reclaimed the area that mankind had so briefly occupied.

Lessons to be learned from the Civil War

The American troops in Iraq faced many difficult problems. They were often ambushed by snipers shooting from behind barriers, from windows and doorways, etc. The enemy often shot at Americans and then quickly disappeared into the crowds where there was no way to distinguish an enemy from an ordinary Iraqi citizen.

This kind of war has baffled military leaders throughout history, especially in modern times. There are no recognized rules for fighting this kind of war. How does the military respond to an attack where large numbers of non-combatants may be killed?

The American Civil War experiences may be helpful in solving this kind of problem.

In February 1862 a Union army moved southward capturing Fort Heiman, Fort Henry and the area around the mouth of the Tennessee River. A few days later, Union gunboats started up the Tennessee River. Within a short time all the Confederate gunboats between the Muscle Shoals and the mouth of the Tennessee River had been captured, destroyed, or put out of commission. Union boats moved troops, supplies, and equipment up and down the river below the Muscle Shoals without fear. It appeared that in the area, the Union had won a clear victory over the Confederacy. But not for long.

Confederate sympathizers often acting alone or in small groups and without any official leadership, began attacking the gunboats. These guerrillas would usually hide in the bushes along the riverbank and fire small arms at exposed people on the Union gunboats. Deck hands and soldiers made easy targets. The pilots of the gunboats were preferred targets. The guerrillas' main purpose was to kill an enemy, disrupt normal operations, destroy supplies, etc. Occasionally the guerrillas would actually capture, ransack, and then destroy a gunboat.

Of course the Union gunboats responded to these guerrilla attacks. Union gunners fired cannons into the woods along the riverbanks from which guerrillas were firing. The guerrillas quickly withdrew and merged into the general population. Sometimes a gunboat would land a squadron of mounted horsemen to battle with the guerrillas. This seldom produced any good results. The Union soldiers quickly learned that there was no way to separate the enemy from the non-combatants. Seldom would a local citizen give information about guerrilla activities.

The gunboat commanders called the guerrilla warfare "barbarous" and "uncivilized" and they retaliated in kind.

Union Gunboats During the Civil War

Union Commodore C. H. Davis, who commanded the gunboats on the lower Tennessee River in the autumn of 1862, ordered all gunboats not to tie up to a river bank at any time. Larger guns were to be kept loaded. Small arms were ready to repel snipers and boarders. Any time a vessel was fired on, it was ordered to "fire back with spirit" and to destroy anything in that neighborhood within the reach of the guns. The order also stated that there "is no impropriety in destroying homes" that seems to be offering shelter to the rebels. "Should innocent persons suffer," he wrote, "it will be their own fault." It was generally believed that this policy would teach local citizens that it could be to their advantage to inform Union authorities about guerrilla activities in the area.

Despite these harsh retaliatory tactics by the Union forces, the guerrillas continued to operate throughout the Civil War.

The Army of Tennessee Moves into the Muscle Shoals Area

After the Atlanta campaign of 1864 General John Bell Hood's Confederate Army consisted of about 35000 men and officers. Weak, disillusioned, disorganized, and poorly supplied, this army, the Army of Tennessee, did not have the strength to go on the offensive, but it did have a fairly well defined mission.

Fearing that Union General William Tecumseh Sherman might move his military force into Alabama and destroy the war industries there, Hood arranged his forces south and west of Atlanta hoping to block any such movement. Also, perceiving that Sherman's army was supplied by a railroad out of Chattanooga to Atlanta, Hood decided to cut these lines. He believed that if Sherman's forces were isolated in Atlanta with inadequate supplies, these forces would have to move northward toward their supply base.

As the days and weeks passed and General Sherman made no movement toward Alabama or any movement northward, Hood and Confederate President Jefferson Davis developed a more grandiose scheme. They conceived the idea of moving their forces northward through Tennessee and into Kentucky. They believed that Sherman would have to move his Union forces back northward to block this threat of an invasion of northern territory.

In terms of conventional warfare, this plan was probably as reasonable as could be devised under the circumstances. Of course it had little impact on General Sherman, who after a few weeks, defied the rules of traditional warfare, cut loose from his supply lines, and marched out of Atlanta to the east coast, living off supplies seized by forging parties from Georgia residents in his path.

In late September 1864, General Hood's Confederate Army began moving out of Georgia into Alabama. The army came over Sand Mountain and on through places such as Sumerville, Decatur, Courtland, and finally to the Muscle Shoals area where Hood established his headquarters in Tuscumbia. In late October 1864, about seven months before the Civil War ended and two months after the fall of Atlanta, Hood began his preparations for the invasion of Union held Tennessee and Kentucky.

General Hood commanded a tired, disillusioned army. One soldier wrote that the army was down in the mouth because of the recent defeat at Atlanta. Even General Hood admitted that there was a shortage of everything. To improve morale, reduce the desertion rate, and generally improve efficiency, a special effort was made to pay the soldiers, many of whom had received no pay for almost a year.

Enormous quantities of supplies had been lost with the fall of Atlanta. Such supplies as were available were gathered mainly from parts of Alabama and Mississippi. To supplement these supplies, soldiers were sent out to local farms to forage for food and supplies. Many soldiers had no shoes. To help meet this need, a group of soldiers were assigned "special duty" with the responsibility to gather leather and rawhide from every possible source to make moccasins for the men who needed shoes.

The Confederate army's food was usually inadequate in supply and dull in quality. Peas, corn, sweet potatoes, cane, and other crops were ready for the fall harvest in many places. Many soldiers acting on their own initiative plundered the fields across North Alabama. One soldier crossing Sand Mountain described the area as a "miserably poor country" but admitted that he had never seen so many persimmons in his life. A group of soldiers found a great corn and pea field near Courtland and "laid in a supply." Sweet potatoes seemed to command much interest. One soldier wrote that he found some great sweet potatoes near Gadsen and took about four bushels.

As the Army of the Tennessee moved into the Tennessee River Valley, the soldiers found that the country was worn out. One soldier wrote that the Tennessee River bottom was fine country but the war had played havoc with it. Great farms were going to ruin.

General Hood's Confederate Army Slaughtered in Tennessee

According to a biographer of General John Bell Hood, his command, the Army of Tennessee, was in shambles when it arrived in the Muscle Shoals area. From his headquarters in Tuscumbia, Hood made plans for his 35,000 man military force to drive the Union forces from Tennessee and Kentucky. He hoped that as he moved northward, Union military units would pull out of the Deep South to block his northward excursion. In preparing for this military operation, he faced many problems.

Supplies were basic. Hood had hoped that the Memphis and Charleston Railroad could bring in supplies from northern Mississippi. But he found that supplies were not nearly as plentiful as expected and that the railroad was in very bad condition. It was totally inoperable east of Cherokee. He needed 300 wagons with proper animals to transport supplies from the railroad terminus to the army as it moved northward. The wagons and mules simply were not available in adequate numbers. In the cold of winter, neither was food available for the animals.

Another problem was getting the army across the Tennessee River. Earlier as Hood had moved westward across north Alabama after the Atlanta campaign, he had planned to cross the Tennessee at Decatur. But the high water led his engineers to advise against that place in favor of crossing near Courtland. But further examination of that stretch of the river removed it from consideration also. Hood then moved on westward to Tuscumbia to await the arrival of his pontoon bridges which he had left behind. Due to flooded creeks and bad roads, the pontoons arrived several days late. At the end of October 1864 one of the soldiers reported that the bridge "stretched nicely and beautifully across the Tennessee."

Many of the problems of the Army of the Tennessee resulted from Hood's own confusion and carelessness. For example, he seldom committed his plans to paper; hence his own staff and his superiors seldom fully understood his thinking. In many cases his superiors were totally uninformed about his actions or plans. On one occasion Hood abandoned his headquarters in Tuscumbia and moved to Florence without informing General P. T. Beauregard, his immediate superior. As a result, an angry Beauregard spent several days trying to locate and communicate with him.

Soldiers Building a Pontoon Bridge (Courtesy of Dorothy McDonald and Robert Steen)

In many respects General Hood was careless or simply did not care at all. For example, shortly after the Battle for Atlanta, his chief of staff was relieved of his duties. No new person was appointed to the position, and the duties were never assigned to anyone of proper rank. Hence administration of matters within the army was very poor. Perhaps a better example involved the pontoon bridges. In moving westward across Alabama, a pontoon bridge was left at the Coosa River which was flooded at the time. The army simply moved on leaving the bridge behind. After a few days General Beauregard observed this fact and had the bridges packed up and shipped off after the departing army.

Despite numerous problems, by November 18th Hood had moved his army across the Tennessee River.

While the Army of Tennessee was being made ready for the northward movement, the soldiers were experiencing life in the Shoals in very different ways. Shortly after arriving in Tuscumbia, a soldier named Sam Wadkins from Columbia, Tennessee, saw a nice sweet potato patch, that looked very tempting. When darkness came, Wadkins and a friend jumped the fence and started grabbing the sweet potatoes. But their labors were quickly interrupted by a loud order to "halt." The foresighted owner had arranged for a guard to protect the potatoes. But that was not to be. Wadkins and his friend ran and escaped safely with a haversack full of potatoes, despite some shooting in their direction.

Wadkins must have thought much about food. He and others were ordered to drive a herd of cattle over the pontoon bridge in preparation for moving into Tennessee. As every cattleman knows, the animals can be unexpectedly stubborn and uncooperative. In this case the lead animals proceeded normally to about the midpoint of the river and then simply stopped and would not move forward. The animals in the rear kept pushing and crowding forward. Many of the animals fell into the river and became entangled with the ropes holding the bridge. The result was that the bridge broke loose from its mooring and many animals drowned. Wadkins' happy conclusion was, "We had beef for supper that night."

Hiram Smith Williams, a soldier from Mobile, had some very different and more pleasant experiences in Florence. Despite being engaged to a girl (whom he later married) back home, he was invited to have tea with some ladies. This pleasant affair led to an invitation to breakfast and several other meals at the home of Mrs. Hugh Thomas.

On November 20, 1864, General John Bell Hood led the Army of Tennessee out of the Muscle Shoals Area into Tennessee. He hoped to capture Nashville and push on into Kentucky. Some historians claim that Hood had no real plan of operation. But he certainly had an objective, approved by President Jefferson Davis and General P. T. Beauregard. He hoped that Union leaders would see his movements as a threat to northern territory and hastily pull troops out of the deep South to stop his northern movement. Such was not to be.

The northward movement started in cold, rainy weather. Several supply wagons bogged down in the mud before getting out of Florence. Yet for many Confederate soldiers this movement with all its hardships was more than a military operation. It was going home. One such Rebel noted, "The ground is frozen hard and a sharp, cold wind is blowing but as my face is toward Tennessee, I feel none of these things." As the army actually entered Tennessee, the troops from the Volunteer State raised a "hearty cheer" and stepped briskly onto their native soil.

The Confederates moved northward against light military resistance through Waynesboro and Lawrenceburg and on through Columbia to Franklin where according to one survivor, "the death angel gathered a rich harvest." In the Battle of Franklin, Hood lost over 5000 men (or about one-sixth of his army) in five hours of battle. One soldier called it the darkest page in the history of the war. Despite heavy Confederate losses, Hood with about 25,000 men, pressed on toward Nashville. The forward progress was slow but involved little military action other than minor skirmishing.

On December 15th the Confederate soldiers could see Nashville. Victory seemed to be in sight, but disaster came. General George H. Thomas , the Union commander, instead of waiting for Hood to attack, slammed 40,000 Union troops into the 25,000 man Confederate Army. The result was a rout. Hood's army dissolved and fled southward in the darkness and rain. All that night Hood's men jammed the road southward abandoning their units, equipment, weapons, and supplies. The massive flight continued through Franklin to Columbia before Hood and his officers could reestablish some organizational structure and offer delaying resistance to the advancing Union forces.

In Columbia, Hood sought the advice of General N. B. Forrest and was bluntly informed that the Confederates could not hold Tennessee and should withdraw south of the Tennessee River where the Union forces could not reach them. Having no real alternative, Hood accepted Forrest's advice. The ill-equipped, scantily clad, poorly fed, and disorganized Confederate troops struggled southward while cavalry units under General Forrest and a special infantry unit tried to delay the advancing Union troops.

The leading units of the Army of the Tennessee reached the Tennessee River on Christmas Day 1864. There was no Christmas celebration, no parties, no hot tasty food and no bridge across the Tennessee River.

Hood selected Bainbridge, about eight miles east of Florence, as the place for the crossing. Two problems were immediately obvious. The flooded river was out of its banks and all the pontoon bridges had been left behind in the hasty retreat. Finally the engineers placed together parts of a bridge that had been captured earlier. This was a risky, unstable structure.

The infantry had to cross single file with three or four feet between each man. Only a few wagons and guns could be on the bridge at any one time. On December 28th the last of the Confederate army crossed the Tennessee River into Colbert (then known as Franklin) County.

This timing was crucial. Union leaders had sent gunboats up the river to disrupt the crossing. These gunboats began shelling the bridge as the last troops were crossing the river.

On this occasion, few if any leisure moments were spent in the Muscle Shoals region. General Hood established a temporary headquarters in Tuscumbia near the home of Mrs. Godley. The Confederate troops were quickly moved on to Corinth, Mississippi.

Hood's Tennessee campaign was a disaster, as figures indicate. Approximately 35,000 men and officers crossed into Tennessee. About five weeks later, on December 31, 1864, Hood had 16, 913 men and 1795 officers present for duty.

As the now rag-tag army moved westward, the residents of the Shoals area saw the last of the Confederate military. Their next view of Confederate soldiers was the returning veterans that came limping home at the end of the war a few weeks later.

But the Muscle Shoals area was not long without a military presence. In early January 1865 the Union military forces reoccupied the Tennessee Valley and continued their control of the area until the war ended three months later.

Yet despite military occupation, social disorganization, and economic hardships throughout the valley, the Muscle Shoals area had one more significant part to play in the Civil War.

Wilson's Raiders Write "Finish" to the Southern Rebellion

As General John Bell Hood was moving his Confederate army out of the Muscle Shoals area in early January 1865, Union General James H. Wilson, the youngest general in the Union army at age 27, was an unhappy camper. He wanted a more exciting and significant military responsibility than occupation duty which seemed to be the only assignment available at the time.

For several months, Wilson had urged his superiors to permit him to organize a major cavalry raid into west-central Alabama. He argued that important industries existed in the areas around Tuscaloosa, Shelby County, Selma, and Montgomery, and that these places had never been touched by military action during the Civil War. Wilson believed that the Confederacy was rapidly coming to an end, and that a raid through these areas of Alabama would cut off essential supplies to the Confederate army.

After the defeat of General Hood's army at Nashville, Wilson again reminded his superiors of his plan and requested permission to prepare for and execute the suggested raid. In early January 1865 he received the authorization to raise and train a major cavalry force to carry out the mission he envisioned. The entire operation is well described in Yankee Blitzkrieg by James Jones.

General Wilson established an assembly point and training camps in west Lauderdale County. He hoped to eventually have five divisions with about 20,000 men under his command. The buildup never reached this number, but by March 1st he commanded the largest cavalry force that had ever been assembled in the western hemisphere. Three divisions were stationed according to the "cantonment plan" near the Tennessee River at Gravelly Springs, while another division was camped near Waterloo. These locations facilitated the bringing in of supplies. According to the cantonment plan, seventy two small cabins to house the men and six long buildings for the horses of each regiment were hastily erected. These structures were located on high, dry ground with plenty of water and easy access to the river.

The military camps were situated well away from population centers such as Florence and Tuscumbia. It therefore received little attention from the local citizens but did not go unnoticed. Wilson reported that for a while, guerrillas and deserters harassed both Union troops and the local citizens. Before serious training could begin, this opposition had to be crushed. Small, swift-moving cavalry units were dispatched throughout the Muscle Shoals region and northeast Mississippi destroying any opposition that could be found. The guerrillas and deserters soon ceased to be a problem.

The local citizens quickly came to resent the Union military. This army, like the Confederate army, had a shortage of food. Hence foraging parties were sent throughout the area gathering food for the men and horses. On one occasion, a Sergeant Pepper wrote in his diary, "The boys got a lot of forage today such as meat, chickens, and corn." But the people in the Shoals area were already impoverished; hence such good fortune was only occasional.

Unfriendly attitudes by local citizens were shown in many ways. On one occasion a Union soldier tried to have "a good sociable chat" with a group of women. He was rebuffed. Later he wrote that he did not care for Southern women.

Gradually Union cavalrymen were gathered from Tennessee and Kentucky. Strict discipline and careful organization, along with constant training, quickly bought the cavalry units into tiptop fighting form.

While the training was in progress, Wilson had scouts roaming all over northwest Alabama. Through their reports, he learned that no significant Confederate military opposition existed anywhere near his proposed route. He also learned that the hill country between the Tennessee Valley and the Black Belt was extremely poor and offered no real opportunity for foraging. Hence, the cavalry units would have to carry food and supplies with them. There would be no living off the land.

With his plans formulated, his men trained, and his supplies in camp, Wilson was ready to move southward across the Tennessee River on March 4th. But his plans were made without consulting the forces of nature. In late February the skies opened and torrential rains came down. The river quickly overflowed its banks. One soldier reported seeing a boat floating in a corn field. Another local citizen claimed that the river was higher than it had been at any time during the past forty years. Many supplies were lost in the rapidly rising waters, and sickness suddenly increased.

Wilson was worried. He informed General U. S. Grant that it was impossible to move the army across the Tennessee River at that time.

On March 12th the rains subsided and the river began receding. The river crossing began two days later at Waterloo. The crossing was delayed again when Confederate snipers started shooting from the south side of the river. Union gunboats were hastily brought in to clear the immediate area of opposition. Then the crossing resumed and continued for the next three days.

At 3:00 a.m. on March 22, 1865, about one month before the war ended, Wilson's cavalry began their march southward out of the Shoals area. His command consisted of 13,480 well-mounted cavalrymen, about 1500 un-mounted men, and 250 supply wagons. Every man carried a Spencer seven-shot repeating carbine and one hundred rounds of ammunition. Each also carried a five-day supply of food. The men and officers were excited. All wanted an easy campaign and expected great accomplishments. General Upton, one of the division commanders, expected the campaign to seal the doom for the Confederacy.

A reader may question the influence of Wilson's raid, but as a military operation it was a major success. Numerous coal mines and ironworks were destroyed, especially in Shelby and Bibb counties. The University of Alabama, an officer training institution, was burned along with several factories in the Tuscaloosa area. During the Civil War, Selma had become the second largest industrial center in the South. Its industrial park was destroyed and much of the town burned. From Selma, Wilson's raiders moved to Montgomery, which surrendered rather than putting up resistance. Alabama's Governor Thomas Watt barely managed to avoid capture by hastily leaving town for Eufaula as the Wilson raiders arrived. After more burning and destroying, the Wilson army moved eastward out of Montgomery into Georgia, where on May 10th they captured the fleeing President of the Confederacy, Jefferson Davis.

This final accomplishment did indeed spell the end of the Confederate States of America.

Part Four: The Post-Civil War Years

Joseph Humphreys Sloss

The South has always had a strong pull on the people who called the area "home". This was most evident during the Civil War years.

Joseph Humphreys Sloss was one of those who felt the strong pull of their homeland.

Sloss was born in Summerville, Alabama but grew up in the Shoals area while his father, Rev. James L. Sloss, was minister at the First Presbyterian Church in Florence. At the age of 18, Joseph Sloss was admitted to the bar after three years of study in his uncle's law office.

Like many young Americans seeking economic opportunity, Sloss moved northward and settled in Edwardville, Illinois. A thriving law practice and active membership in the Democratic Party soon followed.

In 1858 while the famous Lincoln-Douglas Debates in Illinois were gaining national attention, Sloss campaigned for and was elected to the Illinois legislature. From this position he helped defeat Abraham Lincoln and gave his support to his good friend, Stephen A. Douglas who was successfully elected to the U. S. Senate. Two years later when Douglas ran for the presidency, Sloss again supported him. This effort proved unsuccessful and Lincoln was elected president.

When some southern states including Alabama seceded from the Union and formed the Confederate States of America, they reflected Sloss's thinking and values. While not a strong advocate of slavery, Sloss firmly believed that the South had not been treated fairly by northern radicals and the national government.

While war clouds swirled over the nation, Sloss, like hundreds of other Americans, had to choose between the love of his homeland or loyalty to the Union. Faced with the choice, Sloss gave up his many connections to Illinois, packed up his family and moved to Tuscumbia. There he immediately was caught up in the frenzied preparation for war.

As the Civil War got under way, Sloss raised a company of volunteers in Lauderdale County. In October 1862 the company joined with the Fourth Alabama Cavalry which then commanded by Colonel P. D. Roddey of Lawrence County. After Roddey was promoted, the regiment was commanded by Colonel William A. Johnson of Lauderdale County.

Sloss was destined to serve a relatively minor role in the War. He was elected Captain by the men in the company and became the company commander. Later he was promoted to Major and transferred to another unit.

As the military action ceased, Sloss returned to Tuscumbia and started building a new life. He joined with Robert B. Lindsay in establishing a law practice. Lindsay had served in the State Legislature before the war and was later elected governor. Sloss entered local politics and helped reorganize the Democratic Party in Alabama.

In the realm of local politics Sloss served as mayor of Tuscumbia during the reconstruction era. Like many politicians, Sloss needed a voice to reach the public and a business to raise money. This led him to enter the newspaper business in addition to his other activities. He established the Tuscumbia Times which was later merged with the North Alabamian and became known as the North Alabamian and Times.

Apparently Sloss never seriously considered returning to Illinois after the Civil War. Despite many hardships for him and his family, the South and the Muscle Shoals area were always his home.

Samuel R. Lowery, an American Attorney

When slavery was abolished after the Civil War, about four million people gained their freedom. Equally important, their long-suppressed energies and creative talents were liberated. One such man was Samuel R. Lowery. He became the first African-American from the South to practice law before the United States Supreme Court.

Samuel's father, Peter Lowery, was in early life a slave. He worked hard at several jobs, became a skilled craftsman and earned enough money to buy freedom for himself and several members of his family. He married a free Indian woman, Ruth Mitchell, and Samuel was their first born son in 1832 in Nashville, Tennessee. Peter Lowery became an Elder in the Disciples of Christ and served as pastor of a church in Nashville form 1849 to 1866. After acquiring a good education, Samuel followed in his father's footsteps and became a minister. He also taught school for a period of time. During the Civil War, he served as a chaplain for the 9th U.S. Colored Artillery Battalion.

After the close of the Civil War, Lowery began reading law in the office of a white attorney and was soon admitted to the bar. In a short time he was practicing law before the Supreme Court of Tennessee and in the Federal Courts of North Alabama.

In 1880 Mrs. Belva Lockhart (the first woman to practice law before the U. S. Supreme Court) vouched for Lowery's qualifications and good character and requested that he be admitted to practice before the court. The request was honored, and Lowery argued his first case before the Court about two years later.

After slavery was abolished, most ex-slaves lived in poverty. Lowery's own family was no exception. He blamed the "cotton culture" for much of the hardship people suffered and eagerly sought ways of improving the economic conditions in the South.

Samuel moved to Huntsville, Alabama in 1875. He continued to practice law, but more importantly he established the Lowery Industrial Academy. He traveled over the Tennessee Valley urging people to start producing silk through the growth of mulberry bushes and silk worms. He believed that the silk culture could replace or at least supplement cotton in Alabama. A major goal of his was providing jobs with good wages for women and children.

Lowery's own daughters, Ruth and Anna, are sometimes called the "foundresses of silk culture in Alabama." They operated the Academy for a short time in Huntsville. Poor women were introduced to sewing, knitting, and needlework with silk thread.

The silk industry never caught on in Alabama, but for many years mulberry trees dotted the landscape as a result of their efforts.

William Hooper Council, an African-American Educator

Many prominent black men and women have exercised great influence in Alabama. One such man, William Hooper Council, was a powerful force in shaping the history of the Tennessee Valley.

Council was born a slave in North Carolina on July 12, 1848. At the age of nine, he, his mother and his brother, were sold through the Richmond Slave Pens to David C. Humphreys of Huntsville, Alabama. The Councils remained with Humphreys until emancipation, working mainly the corn and cotton fields of Jackson County. In 1864 while the Civil War was in progress, the Council family went north where William's mother and brother died. After slavery was abolished, William Council, at the age of seventeen, returned to the Tennessee Valley.

Education was always a central part of Council's life and work. He had very little formal education. A few weeks in the classroom followed by irregular study under several tutors gave him a smattering of an education.

With this foundation plus a thirst for knowledge and a willingness to work hard, Council built a life of real achievements despite many hardships. At various times he was a newspaper editor, a writer, an ordained minister, a school teacher, and a college president. He passed the state bar examination but never practiced law. In later life, he was awarded an honorary doctorate of philosophy for his outstanding service to humanity.

In 1872, after some years as a farmer, a laborer, and a school teacher, Council was appointed enrolling clerk of the Alabama Legislature. While in this position he joined with others in securing the passage of an act creating a state normal school in the Huntsville area. Council took a competitive examination "with college taught men" and as a result became the principal of this school which opened May 1, 1875. In 1885 the name was changed to Alabama Agricultural and Mechanical College. For the remainder of his life, with the exception of one year, he was principal and then president of this institution.

In this position, Council was able to act on his belief that the future of black and white people depended upon education. Long before Booker T. Washington became well known, Council advocated vocational education as the best way for black people to achieve economic security and advancement in a harsh and unfriendly world. Council never missed an opportunity to promote education. And he worked tirelessly to build Alabama A & M College. Through his work between 1875 and 1909, the door of educational opportunity was opened to thousands of young men and women in the Tennessee Valley, who otherwise would have had little chance of advancement.

Many Alabamians supported Council's educational views but few people, especially blacks, would follow his political leadership.

Immediately after the Civil War, Council, like most black Alabamians, joined the Republican Party. In 1874 when the Democratic Party regained control of the state, Council realized that white Democrats controlled the destiny of black Alabamians. At that time he joined the Democratic Party and remained loyal to it for the remainder of his life. As a Democrat, he had some influence with the party and government leaders, but was politically estranged from the majority of the black Alabamians, who remained loyal to the Republican Party.

Speaking to mainly a black audience in Tuscumbia in 1880, he described the existing political situation and predicted the future: "If you do not make friends of and unite with the white people among whom you live, on all questions touching on our civil and political welfare, you will regret it in time to come. It will not be 25 years before the white people of this country, if they have found that you go in masses against them right or wrong, on all political questions, will come into power and take from you the ballot which you continue to cast against them. The Republican Party will grow tired of you, and seek to unload the Negro Element, and like the bat which was disowned by the beast and not recognized by the birds, you will find favor with neither Democrats nor Republicans."

While the words of Mr. Council were not well received, they turned out to be true. The Republican Party was soon under the control of a "Lily White Faction" which wanted to exclude blacks. And within twenty one years, the Democrats adopted the Constitution of 1901 under the terms of which, black Alabamians lost the right to vote.

William H. Council was a difficult man to understand. Part of his philosophy of life and education was that every person's growth must begin where he is right now and not from where he would like to be. Council saw black Alabamians not as a people who had great social, political, and economic power, but a people at the bottom of the ladder. This was a position Council understood well. He once wrote: "I have slept in a cotton pen a whole winter because I had no better place. I have washed an only shirt and then sat in the shade of a tree while it dried. I wore a pair of 'Yankee' drawers for pants a whole winter. I wore low cut shoes in the winter without socks. When a boy, I never had an undershirt nor dreamed of an overcoat. I plowed, once three days for an old Greenleaf's Arithmetic. I only had split cedar for light for three years. Later I walked eight miles, three times a week, for three lessons a week in physics and chemistry and paid a learned professor 50 cents for each lesson. God forbid that anybody, white or black, should ever be forced to battle against such odds."

Whether people today appreciate William H. Council may not matter much. But thanks to his work, life in the Tennessee Valley is a little bit better for all of us.

Jesse and Frank James – Their Connection with the Muscle Shoals Area

Robbery, theft of property, and other forms of crime have been a part of life in the Muscle Shoals area. Most of these crimes have stimulated very little public interest. But the robbery of the Muscle Shoals Canal payroll was one major exception.

In 1881 the Muscle Shoals Canal was under construction by the U. S. Army Corp of Engineers. Several camps had been established about four miles apart over the entire length of the Muscle Shoals. The construction was under the supervision of military engineers. A large workforce lived in these camps while clearing the terrain, digging the canal, and building locks. Life for the workers was hard and dangerous, but the pay was good.

On March 11, 1881, Alexander G. Smith, paymaster for the workers at the Bluewater Camp, located near the mouth of Bluewater Creek, rode about twenty miles into Florence to pick up the payroll money. He picked up $5240.80 in gold and silver coins and some currency from the William T. Campbell Banking Company. Smith left the bank, traveled down Court Street and then eastward beside the canal toward the Bluewater Camp.

About two miles from the camp he dismounted from his horse to open a gate. When he dismounted, three men rode up, pointed their hand guns at him, and took the federal government money he was carrying. They also took Smith's personal money, a watch, and several personal items. The bandits then forced Smith to ride northward with them toward the Tennessee State Line.

Later in the afternoon, with rain falling and strong winds blowing, the bandits stopped and divided the government money they had taken from Smith. They returned Smith's personal money and property to him. Then he was permitted to start back to the Bluewater Camp, while the robbers continued northward into Tennessee.

Smith arrived back at the camp early the following morning, and reported the robbery to Major William R. King, camp commander. A mounted posse was hurriedly sent after the robbers and followed them well into Tennessee before admitting failure and returning home. Local law enforcement officials in north Alabama and southern Tennessee were notified by the telegraph of the robbery. Local lawmen were requested to be on the lookout for the bandits.

For the next few days nothing happened. All hope of capturing the bandits and recovering the money seemed lost.

Then the big break came. On March 26th, fifteen days after the robbery, a stranger claiming to be Tom Hill, walked into a saloon in Whites Creek, a village in the Nashville, Tennessee area. Within a short time he was drunk, sick and creating a ruckus. Local men subdued him and turned him over to Nashville law enforcement authorities. It was soon discovered that his real name was William Ryan and that he was a member of the Jesse and Frank James gang. Ryan, alias Tom Hill, was carrying nearly $1500 in gold and currency. This immediately brought him under suspicion, but he denied any knowledge of the Muscle Shoals Canal payroll robbery.

Major King and Alexander G. Smith traveled to Nashville, where Smith identified Ryan as one of the robbers. King confiscated the gold that Ryan was carrying.

The authorities also learned from Ryan that Jesse and Frank James had been living with their families in the outskirts of Nashville for the preceding six years. Jesse was known in the local area as J. D. "Tom" Howard and Frank was known as B. J. "Ben" Woodson. They were generally considered by their neighbors to be quiet and orderly, law-abiding citizens. But the neighbors did notice that they loved horse racing and were often absent from home for extended periods of time.

The James brothers were not available for questioning. When they began to be connected with the Muscle Shoals Canal robbery, the brothers hurriedly left Tennessee and returned to their homes in Missouri. William Ryan was returned to Missouri to stand trial for crimes he had committed there. He was soon spending time in prison.

Federal marshals in Missouri arrested James A. "Dick" Liddell, another member of the James gang, for crimes he had committed in Missouri. When questioned, Liddell claimed to be innocent of the Muscle Shoals Canal robbery but stated that Jesse and Frank James and William Ryan actually committed the crime.

Law enforcement authorities in Alabama and Tennessee, along with the general public, believed the James gang committed the Muscle Shoals Canal robbery, but there seemed little chance of bringing them to justice.

Back in Alabama, Major King reported to the Secretary of War, Robert Lincoln, son of President Abraham Lincoln, that he had no money left to offer a reward; hence there was little chance of recovering the stolen money.

This robbery had stimulated very little local interest until the names of Jesse and Frank James were brought forth as major suspects. Then several people in the Elgin Crossroads/Rogersville area who operated boarding houses, saloons, and other businesses, remembered seeing and serving three men during the days before the robbery.

There seemed to be little chance of bringing any of the Jesse and Frank James gang to justice for the Muscle Shoals Canal robbery. But conditions were changing. Federal law enforcement and justice officials became involved. The wheels of justice were slowly turning in north Alabama.

The federal district attorney in Huntsville was busy collecting evidence against the major suspects. This evidence was turned over to a grand jury, which brought indictments against William Ryan and Jesse and Frank James, accusing them of the Muscle Shoals Canal payroll robbery. David Liddell was indicted for complicity in the robbery.

The trial of these accused men was flawed from the beginning. Jesse James (Mr. J. D. Howard) was already dead, having been shot in the back by Robert Ford, a "friend" and fellow gang member. William Ryan was serving time in the Missouri prison for crimes committed in Missouri. David Liddell was brought to Huntsville, tried, and found guilty of complicity in the Muscle Shoals Canal payroll robbery. The judge delayed sentencing in order to get his testimony against Frank James, who had been arrested in Missouri and returned to Huntsville for trial.

The trial of Frank James for the Muscle Shoals Canal payroll robbery was one of the most noted trials in Alabama history. The defense attorney was Leroy Pope Walker, a popular Alabama lawyer and a former Confederate general and Confederate Secretary of War. He was assisted by two prominent lawyers from Huntsville and Nashville. The prosecuting attorney was William H. Smith, a former Republican governor of Alabama.

The trial began on April 16, 1884. A jury was selected in the morning with Walker and Smith quarreling constantly and arguing over legal technicalities, much to the enjoyment of a packed courtroom.

Numerous witnesses were called during the three-day trial. The prosecuting attorney called several witnesses, including Alexander G. Smith, all of whom claimed to have seen Frank James in Lauderdale County in the days prior to the robbery. But not one of these witnesses could positively identify Frank James as one of the men they had seen immediately before and during the robbery. The defense attorney had better luck. Walker called several witnesses that vouched for the good character of Frank James. Still other witnesses swore that they had seen James in Nashville, talked with him and had done business with him on the day of the robbery.

All during the trial, the prosecuting attorney tried to portray Frank James as a vicious criminal who had committed numerous crimes against many innocent people. On the other hand, Walker, the defense attorney, portrayed James as a good loyal Southern gentleman who had risked his life many times during the Civil War fighting for the South.

Frank and his family helped create the impression that he was a southern gentleman rather than a western outlaw. Frank's wife, Anne, and their six-year-old son, attended all sessions of the trial and conducted themselves in a very friendly, pleasing manner. Frank was probably the best dressed man at the trial. He wore a Prince Albert coat and played the role of a friendly, likeable southerner at all times.

Public sympathy in the Huntsville area was strongly in favor of Frank's acquittal. Gifts of fruit and flowers arrived at the jail for him every morning during the trial from some unidentified source.

One historian has stated that when the trial was over, the jury of "twelve ex-Confederates solemnly left the courtroom and returned shortly with smiles on their faces" and announced a "not guilty" verdict. Actually the jury was out for four hours before the "not guilty" verdict was pronounced. Apparently the trial jury took two votes. During the first vote three members believed Frank James was guilty of the robbery. But after further discussion, the jury voted unanimously "not guilty."

The ordeal was over; Frank James was a free man. This was the end of the James Gang. The Muscle Shoals Canal payroll robbery was never solved. Frank James returned to Missouri and lived an exemplary life until his death in 1915.

But the people of the Muscle Shoals area would not let the stories about Jesse and Frank James and the Muscle Shoals Canal payroll robbery die.

Over the years several people have told stories about the activities of the James brothers in the area just prior to the robbery. According to these stories, Jesse and Frank spent time in boarding houses, stores, and saloons.

The James brothers did have relatives in the Muscle Shoals area. One story claims that after the robbery, Jesse and Frank visited these relatives in the Freedom Hills area for several days.

There has been a tendency for many people in the Muscle Shoals area, and across the nation, to see the James brothers as Robin Hood types. A few years ago, a popular storyteller thrilled his audience with a story that after the robbery, Jesse and Frank rode westward through Florence and at one point met an elderly gentleman who was suffering in great need. The story goes that Jesse helped the man with a generous gift from the money he had recently stolen.

Other stories abound. One gentleman in his old age got his stories mixed up and claimed that he personally saw Jesse and Frank James rob the Campbell Bank in Florence. He described in great detail how the robbers came out of the bank, climbed on their horses, fired shots into the air, and "skedaddled out of town." Actually the bank was never robbed.

Another story describes how the James brothers robbed the stagecoach coming into Florence from Huntsville. This incident never happened.

A short time ago, an elderly man sidled up to Lee Freeman, librarian in the Florence-Lauderdale Public Library and stated that he knew the location of the secret burial place of Frank James up in Tennessee. He seemed crestfallen and a little unbelieving when Lee informed him that Frank James had become in later life a very respected citizen who was buried after a public funeral in Missouri upon his death on February 18, 1915.

Jesse Owens, a National Hero

James Cleveland Owens, a native of northwest Alabama, is remembered for winning four gold medals in the 1936 Olympics and a life of public service after his athletic success.

Owens was born in the Oakville community of Lawrence County on September 13, 1913. He was the 13th child of a sharecropper family and was the grandson of a former slave. In the first few years of life, he experienced the poverty, poor health, inadequate schools, and limited opportunity which characterized conditions in Alabama at that time for tenant farmers especially black tenant farmers.

The Owens family was not typical. This family, especially Owens's mother, was determined to find a better way of life for her family. As a result of this determination, the family moved to Cleveland, Ohio in about 1922. This move was part of the "Black Migration" which carried over two million Black Americans out of the rural agricultural Southland to northern industrial-urban areas. Later in life Owens explained that his family moved northward to find better job opportunities, better schools for the kids, and reduced racial violence. The move brought immediate success for the Owens.

In Cleveland, Owens entered the East Technical High School. There he found a "new world" and a new name. Back in the Tennessee Valley, James Cleveland was commonly called "J. C." His teachers misunderstood this to be "Jesse". Hence, he became widely known for the remainder of his life as "Jesse Owens."

Despite poor health, Jesse always enjoyed athletics, especially running. His talents were recognized by his high school coach, Charles Riley, who became his inspiration and motivator. By the time he graduated from high school he was well known nationally in athletic circles, having established three national records in track and jumping.

Success followed him to Ohio State University which he entered on an athletic scholarship. In May 1935, during a Big 10 meet, Owens established three new world records in less than two hours as a member of the OSU team. He completed the 220 yard dash in 20.3 seconds, 220 yard low hurdles in 22.6 seconds, and the broad jump for 26 feet and 8 ¼ inches.

Jesse was never an outstanding student in the classroom but he loved athletics and loved competition. Long before the 1936 Olympic Games started in Berlin Germany, he saw this as the pinnacle of his amateur career. As a competitor in the Olympics, Jesse

Owens won four gold medals and set three new world records. Medals were won in the 100 meter dash (10.2 sec.), the long jump (26 ft. 5 ¼ inch), 200 meter dash (20.7 seconds), and the first leg of the 400 meter relay (39.8 sec)

Jesse's success was not accidental nor did it come easy. From early in life Jesse Owens adopted a life style that served him well. He liked people, enjoyed their company and people liked him. In a world filled with racism, he was never burdened with a chip on his shoulder and self-doubts.

He was well aware that unusual and unnecessary obstacles made difficult his road to success. But he was not a quitter. Jesse Owens was always a hard worker. He quickly grasped the opportunities that were available to him rather than cry foul and take the easy road to failure. Jesse travelled down the hard road to success when nearly all the arrows pointed in the other direction.

Today Jesse Owens is a well-known figure in northwest Alabama. Such was not the case in 1936. The two local newspapers at the time did not mention Jesse Owens. In fact they barely mentioned the Olympics at all. One paper did mention Cornelius Johnson, the first Black American to win a gold medal in the Olympics. This medal was won with the high jump (6 ft. 8 inches) the day before Owens won his first medal.

Winning four gold medals in the 1936 Olympics was the defining point of Jesse Owens' life. From that point on most of his personal and professional life was built on this success.

Adolph Hitler, the Nazi, Jew-hating dictator of Germany, had a major influence on Jesse's life. Hitler had met and personally congratulated the first gold medal winner (a German) at the 1936 Olympics in Berlin, Germany but had discontinued the practice when informed by Olympic officials that he must greet all or none of the winners. Therefore when Cornelius Johnson, a black American, won a gold medal he was not greeted by Hitler and the following day when Jesse Owens won medals, he like the other winners at the time, was not greeted.

This situation probably would have been forgotten except that the New York Times ran a headline story suggesting that Hitler had not greeted the American blacks because he considered them, along with the Jews, to be inferior to the "superior Aryan race." A black newspaper in Cleveland, Ohio published essentially the same story with emphasis on Hitler's failure to greet Jesse Owens. It thus created the impression that Hitler had deliberately snubbed Owens because he was black. Other papers picked up on this story and soon Americans all over the country came to believe that Hitler had deliberately snubbed only Jesse Owens. Thus, Jesse Owens became one of the best known blacks in America because he had won four gold medals and because Hitler had insulted him.

In recounting his Olympic experiences, Jesse Owens sometimes told audiences that Hitler would not shake his hand. On numerous other occasions he never mentioned the incident. One writer suggested that Owens knew that he had not been insulted any more than other Olympic winners, but that he recounted the myth when it was to his advantage to do so.

While Americans, black and white, were generally upset over the "snubbing of an American hero," Jesse took it in stride. He was well aware that Americans were not free from racial prejudice. He once told an audience, "After all the stories about Hitler and the snub, I came back to my native country and I couldn't ride in the front of the bus. I wasn't invited to shake hands with Hitler, but I wasn't invited to the White House to shake hands with the President either."

In 1937 Jesse Owens graduated from OSU and faced the difficult probability of securing employment in the depression era. In 1938, Jesse stated it would be correct to say he was "a hero yesterday" and "nobody today." That was not totally accurate. He was able to build a successful life on his Olympic successes.

But life was hard and economic success came slowly. On one occasion, he raced a race horse in the 100 yard dash and won. Later, when informed that racing a horse was degrading, he asked, "What was I supposed to do? I had four gold medals, but you can't eat four gold medals. There was no television, no big advertising, no endorsements back then. At least not for a black man anyway."

Over the next years, Owens engaged in a wide variety of business and entertainment activities. Movie making, night club appearances, and lecturing consumed much of his time. He endorsed and helped advertise numerous products. These activities never brought great wealth, but he did earn a good living which he enjoyed to the fullest.

His national popularity continued. In a 1950 poll of sportswriters, he was named the world's "top track performer" since 1900.

Owens spent much time performing volunteer work for non-profit causes. In 1955, he conducted a highly popular good will tour of India for the State Department.

As the Civil Rights Movement in the U. S. was winding down, he wrote a partially autobiographical book entitled, <u>Blackthink, My Life as Black Man and White Man</u>. Owens defined "blackthink" as "pro-Negro, anti-white." He made clear his condemnation of "blackthink."

Jesse Owens's life after 1936 reflected his success in the Olympics. But his influence as a role model was as broad as his athletic achievements. His many good works were recognized when President Gerald Ford presented him with the Presidential Medal of Freedom. Later, President Jimmy Carter awarded him the Living Legends Award in 1979.

Jesse Owens died on March 31, 1980, from lung cancer after years of smoking.

The Old Railroad Bridge

The Old Railroad Bridge, sometimes called the Florence and Tennessee River Bridge, has touched the lives of most citizens of the Muscle Shoals area. The Bridge is in reality a symbol of man's struggle to build a better life and a better community in the Shoals area.

When settlers first moved into the area in the early 1800s, crossing the river was a major problem. The river was too large to be forded without great danger. Hence ferries were established as one of the first kinds of business in the area. Some, such as the Colbert Ferry, Lamb's Ferry, Cheatham's Ferry and others became well known. But the ferries were slow, expensive, and inconvenient. Early settlers in the area dreamed of a bridge over the river.

The first bridge across the Tennessee River in the Shoals area was at Bainbridge about twelve miles upriver from Florence. Construction was barely complete before flood waters swept the wooden structure away.

The Florence Bridge was completed and opened to foot and wagon traffic as a toll bridge in 1840. For the next fourteen years, the bridge was the best way for a traveler to cross the Tennessee River. But in 1854 the destructive forces of nature destroyed two spans of the bridge forcing a reestablishment of the ferry system of crossing the river in Florence.

In the 1850s the bridge at Florence was purchased by the Memphis and Charleston Railroad. It was rebuilt, improved, and reopened to the public again in 1857. This Railroad Bridge had a lower deck for foot and wagon traffic and an upper deck for the movement of trains across the river. But this "modern structure" was short lived. In 1862 as the Union army was pushing its way into the Shoals area. The Confederate military forces burned the bridge to slow the Yankee progress. The ferry was reestablished and operated irregularly until 1870.

Five years after the Civil War ended the Railroad Bridge was rebuilt and reopened to the public. It functioned as before the Civil War. In the 1890s heavy railroad traffic caused part of the bridge to collapse forcing another temporary return to the ferry. The Bridge was hastily rebuilt and greatly strengthened with steel and concrete.

Railroad Bridge Carries Train and Foot Traffic (Courtesy Robert Steen)

Other improvements were needed to keep up with modern progress. The introduction of the electric street car in the early 1900s necessitated electric poles and appropriate wires which were installed about 1904.

Many of our older citizens can remember crossing the Tennessee River by way of the Old Railroad Bridge. They tell interesting tales of walking or riding a wagon or early automobile over the one lane lower deck of the toll bridge. Equally interesting and sometimes more thrilling tales can be told about riding the train or an open street car over the upper deck of the bridge.

The desire for progress and a better way of life that brought the Florence Bridge into existence in 1840 also carried it out of common use almost exactly 100 years later. In December 1940 the O'Neal Bridge became a convenient toll-free bridge. Wagon and automobile traffic was discontinued. Trains continued to use the bridge until 1988.

A large part of the Railroad Bridge which still stands today is a symbol of the successful struggle to build and enjoy a better way of life.

Railroad Travel from Florence

In earlier days when railroads were a prominent means of travel, Florentines complained that they had to go through Tuscumbia in order to travel in any direction.

The inconvenience suffered by the Lauderdale Countians started in the 1850s, when the Memphis and Charleston Railroad built a main line in through Tuscumbia with a spur line to Florence. The M & C RR acquired ownership of the Florence Bridge. It was renovated and rebuilt so that trains as well as other forms of traffic could use it. In 1857 the first train rolled into Florence.

This service was brought about partially through the cooperation of the Florence Mayor and Aldermen. Two acres of land near the south end of Court Street was provided for the depot. The city also agreed to grade the area and maximize the road leading to the depot. To further encourage railroad construction in Florence, it was given a right of way "through, over, and across all public streets" except Court Street.

A new day had dawned. Passengers could board a "transfer train" in Florence and travel to Tuscumbia where they could transfer to a train on the main line. The M & C proudly advertised that passengers could make good connections when traveling in any direction. Also, baggage could be checked in Florence through to all points.

But the service was short lived. The railroad service was completely disrupted by the Civil War, and then the bridge was destroyed.

Shortly after the Civil War, rail service was restored to South Florence before the bridge was rebuilt. Florentine travelers crossed the river by ferry to South Florence and began the rail journey there. In 1870 the M & C RR advertised that a person could eat breakfast in Florence, cross the river on the ferry, and travel by rail to Tuscumbia in time to board trains going north, south, east, or west.

Tuscumbia was an important place in railroad travel. Trains on the main line stopped there giving passengers time for food and refreshments. The Franklin House, later known as the Parshall Hotel was operated by R. K. Craft. He became known for "keeping a first class table and giving good satisfaction" to travelling customers.

The Railroad Bridge of Florence returned to service in 1870 and continued in use for the next twenty-two years despite many near accidents.

Railroad Bridge Rests on Original Foundation (Courtesy Robert Steen)

In 1892 the Railroad Bridge collapsed into the Tennessee River. Rail service was resumed to South Florence while travelers crossed the Tennessee River by the best means possible.

Crossing the river was expensive, difficult, and dangerous. It was "fun for those who liked it, but was hard for the timid." One writer claimed that a traveler in Florence would have to pay twenty-five cents for a carriage ride to the river and an additional twenty-five cents if he had a trunk. A rowboat ride across the Tennessee would cost a dime, but the trunk would cost twenty-five cents. A heavy trunk would cost an additional twenty-five cents.

With pressure from the Alabama Railroad Commission, competing railroad lines and public opinion, the Memphis and Charleston Railroad hurriedly returned the Florence Bridge to service after the 1892 collapse.

Collapse of the Old Railroad Bridge

At about 9 a.m. Friday May 6, 1892, the transfer train from Tuscumbia to Florence was approaching the south end of the Florence Bridge which today is often called the "Old Railroad Bridge." Crossing the Bridge was dangerous. The bridge had been condemned for several years. Maintenance and repairs had been minimal since the bridge had been rebuilt after the Civil War in 1870. Also as technology advanced and industry grew in Florence, the engines, cars, and freight had greatly increased in weight.

Most people expected the Bridge to collapse at some point in time but the trains continued to run. At least four trains crossed the bridge daily with "its precious cargo of human souls" and an ever increasing amount of freight.

On this particular morning the powerful steam engine was pushing three cars and pulling nine others. Five of the cars were loaded with coke and seven were filled with rocks. Engineer Tom Clem eased the train onto the bridge. As the front of the train reached the end of the second span, 150 feet long, a loud thunderous splintering crash was heard. The engine and five cars plunged sixty feet into the swift murky waters of the Tennessee River.

The engine fell first, settling on its side with a corner of the cab and a few inches of smokestack projecting from the water. The five cars fell in a confused mass around the engine but not on it. Some rested on their end while others were turned bottom upwards.

The entire bridge span was completely gone. It lay on the river bed, a twisted, splintered mass of timbers and iron nails.

Seven cars were left standing on the track, one at the very brink of the chasm.

Five Tuscumbians made up the crew. All experienced miraculous escape in the face of what appeared to be certain death.

When bystanders "saw that awful plunge," they quickly rowed small boats to the wreckage. Clem, with a broken shoulder, crawled through the window of the cab into the boat and was quickly followed by the fireman, Frank Jones, who suffered some minor internal injuries. Jack Hamlet, a brakeman, was picked up "more dead than alive" from a car which had fallen bottom upwards. He suffered a broken arm, a leg broken in two places, and a dislocated shoulder. Conductor Bob Plemens, in the front of the train, saw the engine going down and made a "wonderful escape" by jumping unhurt to the roadbed. Will Pyrtle, another brakeman, was on the rear of the train and escaped unhurt.

The injured men were carried to homes of their friends in South Florence where several physicians treated them.

The Memphis and Charleston Railroad Company reacted quickly. The day after the wreck several hundred workmen were busily engaged in removing the wreckage and putting up a temporary span. But several months of renovation and rebuilding on the old foundations occurred before trains could return to Florence.

Streetcar Celebration in Florence

Eight thousand people participated in the "Spirit of Freedom" celebration on July 4th, 2000. Long before the words "Spirit of Freedom" came into common use, Florentines celebrated Independence and many other important events on July 4th.

On July 4th, 1904, amid shouts, gunshots, firecrackers, and the waving of banners and flags, a crowd of about 5000 welcomed the first electric railway streetcar into Florence. The streetcar came over the two-tiered Railroad Bridge from Sheffield and slowly followed the tracks into Florence. At 3:30 p.m. the vehicle came to a stop in front of the Lauderdale County Courthouse. The band stopped playing and the Wheeler Rifles welcomed the new form of transportation with a three-volley salute which was followed by the roar of a cannon fired by the local militia.

Streetcar Serves The Muscle Shoals Area (Courtesy of Richard Sheridan)

There was a strong feeling that a new era was dawning in the Tri-Cities area. In preparation for this new era, Florence was well decorated. Public buildings, stores, and offices all along Court and Tennessee Streets were decorated with flags, bunting, and banners. A large sign stating WELCOME TO THE SHEFFIELD COMPANY hung across Court Street.

The rapid growth of industry in Sheffield and East Florence had created a workforce that often lived in one city and worked in another. The electric streetcar system, owned and operated by the Sheffield Company, provided an efficient and cheap means of travelling from home in one town to the job in another. Congressman William Richardson caught the spirit of the occasion by claiming that the Tri-Cities were no longer separate entities but were now joined together socially and economically.

Alabama's U. S. Senator John Tyler Morgan expanded this theme of unity and predicted that the Shoals area, with all its transportation advantages on the Tennessee River, would complete for commerce with places like Memphis, St. Louis, and Cincinnati.

In the speech making that followed the arrival of the first streetcar J. W. Worthington, President of the Sheffield Company, garnered most of the praise for this new technological marvel. The electric urban railway system, as a means of linking the three towns together, was his idea and it was pushed to fruition by his "indomitable energy and shrewd business tact." But he graciously gave credit to others, especially George and Henry Parsons, who financed the project to the tune of $750,000, and Col. A. B. Andrews who arranged for the use of the railway bridge over the Tennessee River.

The urban railway was headquartered in Sheffield but followed a route through Sheffield, Tuscumbia, and Florence covering a distance of about twelve miles. In Florence the railway, when complete, came up Court Street and proceeded northward to Seven Points. It then turned eastward into the industrial area of East Florence and then returned to the Tennessee River Bridge.

The streetcar system was not new to the area. The system had been operating in Sheffield and Tuscumbia several years before it was reorganized and extended into Florence.

The urban railway system was purchased by the Alabama Power Company in 1925 and discontinued operation on February 3, 1933, in the midst of the Great Depression and with growth of better streets, roads, and automobiles.

The Elk River Bridges

The means of transportation have always been important to the people in the Muscle Shoals area. And major improvements called for celebrations.

On July 2, 1876, over three thousand people gathered on the Judge James Horton plantation to celebrate the opening of the first bridge across the Elk River. The northwest corner of Limestone County lay north and west of Elk River. The settlers in this "Over Elk" region were sometimes isolated from Athens, the county seat by bad weather and flooded rivers. Normal commerce and county business was often disrupted.

The opening of this one-lane wooden bridge called for a major celebration. Nearly 3000 people gathered for the day-long celebration. The "pre-dinner hours" were filled with music by Hector Lane and Ben Sowell and traditional songs such as "The Burial of Sir John Moore" and "John Anderson, My Jo John." Dancing stimulated hearty appetites. A basket of food was brought from every household and spread on hastily improvised tables. One writer wrote, "The long tables groaned beneath the weight of every delicious editable."

In the afternoon, music and dancing continued along with political speeches. Candy was generously distributed to all children.

Judge James Horton who played a major role in this celebration, later gained national fame but suffered major setbacks in local popularity for his decisions in the Scottsboro trials over which he presided.

For many years after Limestone County was created in 1818 the only way to cross Elk River was by fording it in shallow places. William L. McDonald in his recent book, A Walk Through The Past, states that the first ferry on the Elk River was authorized in 1835. Other ferries were put into operation but this service made travel expensive.

The second bridge over Elk River was opened in 1892 at the Elk River Mills. This too, was a one-lane wooden structure but it was more convenient and cheaper than the ferry it replaced. The ferry was operated by Isham and W. B. Vaughn. Pedestrians paid five cents to cross the Elk on this ferry and twenty five cents was paid for teams pulling a wagon.

These early crude bridges ended more than geographical isolation. Many of the early settlers of Limestone traced their ancestry back to the highlands of Scotland. Their ancient customs, traditions, and speech lived on strong in the hills and hollows of the "Over Elk" region. The sounds of fiddle, banjo, and dulcimer were also familiar to the area. The bridges blended cultures while stimulating travel and commerce.

The Elk River Mills Bridge suffered greatly from floods and heavy traffic. After many delays it was replaced with a modern two-lane bridge. Named the Milt Grisham Bridge, it was dedicated on August 2, 1956. This event, like the opening of the first bridge, was celebrated with barbecue, music and merriment, and political speeches.

Tuscumbia Man is Father of Alabama Highway System

William Simpson Keller, half-brother to Helen Keller, has been correctly called the Father of Alabama's highway system.

Modern highway construction began in Alabama in 1911. Through the efforts of Governor Emmett O'Neal of Florence, the legislature passed an act in 1911 creating the Alabama Highway Commission and the position of State Highway Engineer. This engineer was charged with the responsibility of specifying which state roads should be designated trunk or state roads. On April 12, 1911, the Highway Commission at its third meeting, appointed William Simpson Keller to be the State Highway Engineer. He held the position until his death in 1926.

Keller, often called "Uncle Simp" by his family and close friends, was born in Tuscumbia. He was reared and attended public schools in Tuscumbia, graduated from State Normal School in Florence, and in 1893 secured the Bachelor of Civil Engineering Degree from the University of Alabama. By 1911, he was known as one of the foremost road builders in Alabama.

Old Highway on Left; Modern (1920's) Highway Construction on Right

Traditionally in Alabama, road location, construction, and maintenance had resided with the County Commissions. The State Legislature was reluctant to change this. The Highway Act of 1911 appropriated $154,000 annually to be distributed to the counties on a matching basis with the county commissioners specifying which roads would be improved. But in order for a county to secure the state highway money, the highway had to conform to State specifications and be constructed under the supervision of the State Highway Engineer.

Many of the counties were extremely poor and simply did not have revenue from local sources to match the state money. The state constitution imposed severe limits on the amount and nature of local taxes. Also, many counties simply had a very small tax base which consisted mainly of houses and land. About half the counties in Alabama were still using the statutory or free labor system in highway construction. Under that system every man between the age of 18 and 45 had to work a certain number of days on the public road each year.

In order to build a better road, some of the counties began issuing bonds. Madison County led the way in this method of highway financing followed closely by Colbert County and others. Unfortunately many of the early highways were poorly constructed especially with regard to the problem of drainage. Also, most money from the county highway bonds was spent on construction and none reserved for maintenance. As a result many of the county built highways deteriorated rapidly.

In 1919 the Legislature required that a license plate be purchased for each vehicle on the highways. The revenue from this source was earmarked for highway construction. Eighty percent of the revenue was used by the State while twenty percent was distributed among the counties.

Despite a shortage of funds, ignorance of the methods of highway construction and a lack of appreciation for good highways, much progress was made. In 1919 Keller wrote that Alabama could boast of a splendid advancement in highway construction. From practically no improved highways in 1900, Alabama had 9682 miles improved by 1919 and the majority of these improved highways had a hard service.

Others shared this view. About this same time, the U. S. Bureau of Roads published a report indicating that Alabama stood first in the nation in total progress in its highway system.

Shortly after Keller's death from cancer in 1926, the Highway Commission named the bridge on highway 31 across the Tennessee River at Decatur the William Simpson Keller Memorial Bridge. At that time the bridge was under construction. It was completed and opened to traffic on March 6, 1928. Today, a new bridge, the Captain William James Hudson Memorial Bridge, has replaced the seventy year old Keller Memorial Bridge which was torn down in 1998.

A. A. McGregor

Some individuals who make significant and lasting contributions to life in the Muscle Shoals area tend "to fall through the cracks of history" and are seldom remembered. A. A. McGregor was such a man.

In the antebellum era, LaGrange College and Military Academy was located on the top of LaGrange Mountain. Today it is one of the best known historic sites in the Shoals area. The college was opened there by the Methodist Episcopal Church in 1830. The Military Academy was organized and added much later to train military leaders for the South. This institution, which served two different purposes, was destroyed in 1863 during the Civil War by Union military forces. The LaGrange community soon died also. After the institution died and the community faded away, people left and their memories also faded. Its history tended to get lost and forgotten.

A. A. McGregor preserved the story of this educational institution, the community, and many of the people who shared their experiences in that area. This was done in his small book entitled <u>The History Of LaGrange College and Military Academy</u>. The book was written and published in the early 20th century about forty-five years after the Civil War. Today few copies of the work exist anywhere and they are mainly in library collections. Anyone who wants to learn about LaGrange College and Military Academy and its environment will have to examine this book and the many articles also written by McGregor.

Others have written about LaGrange and the educational work going on there but no one could bring the knowledge, talent, and dedication to this project that McGregor could offer.

McGregor was born in Lawrence County, Alabama. After a sound childhood education, he enrolled in LaGrange College in 1849 and graduated in 1854. He was a very knowledgeable and dedicated student. After graduation he stayed on at the college as a professor of mathematics. He served in this position until 1861, at which time he left the teaching profession for service in the Confederate army.

He was a quartermaster officer in units commanded by General Phillip D. Roddey and General Nathan Bedford Forrest. His military service was spent mainly in North Alabama, Mississippi, and Tennessee. While never injured, he had one brother killed and another wounded in the bloody Battle of Franklin in 1864.

When the war was over, McGregor returned home and began life anew as a farmer. But his heart was in the field of education rather than the cotton field. About 1870 he returned to LaGrange and taught a private school "in the old brick church house." After six years he moved to Tuscumbia and took charge of an academy there. In 1885 he became president of the Hartselle College and remained there until his retirement.

Throughout his life McGregor retained fond memories of LaGrange College and his experiences there. These memories led him to become a collector of information about the college and military academy.

About 1900 he shifted from being a collector to a writer. He published numerous articles about the college and military academy. Most of his writings appeared in local newspapers. After the popular "LaGrange Reunion" in 1904, these writing were pulled together, edited, and expanded into his history of LaGrange College.

Thanks to McGregor, a large slice of our local history has been preserved and made available for public use.

LaGrange Reunion

In the summertime many reunions of various groups are common occurrences all over the South. Among the many reunions held in the Shoals, one stands out as an area-wide attraction.

On May 19, 1904, carriages, wagons, saddle horses, and pedestrians made their way up to the top of LaGrange mountain. Former students, faculty, and trustees of LaGrange College and Military Academy were assembling from all over the nation for their first reunion. By 10 a.m. the site was packed with people formerly connected with the college and military academy, and their relatives.

The idea of a reunion came from Mr. Frank R. King, a merchant in Leighton. He and Albert A. McGregor were primarily responsible for a great revival of interest in LaGrange College and for organizing the reunion. King and McGregor wrote dozens of letters and published numerous articles which brought the idea to fruition. King was a prominent amateur historian who organized the Tennessee Valley Historical Society in the 1920s. McGregor was an educator.

The large crowd assembled in and around the "old church on the brow of the hill." The classrooms, dormitories, and other buildings were all gone. Most of the buildings had been destroyed in 1863 by the Union army and the few remaining structures, like the students and faculty, had faded with time.

Mr. Parker N. G. Rand, the only trustee still living, was selected to preside, but due to his feeble condition, Albert McGregor called the assembly to order. Twenty-two former college students and twenty-seven former military cadets were in the audience, along with a few former faculty members.

Many of those assembled had not seen each other for over 42 years. Tears of joy were common as old friends were discovered and as speakers relived earlier, happier days and sad memories. Especially sad were the memories of the many former companions who had fallen during the Civil War. All showed their age and many brought with them scars and injuries suffered in the war. Yet all evidence of suffering could not suppress the joy of reliving old experiences. One writer looking over the crowd wrote, "The old fellows left their harness at home and were boys again for one day."

Those present spoke well for the college and military academy. Most were prominent men in their communities and included planters, educators, judges, ministers, doctors, lawyers, and representatives of other professions.

Probably the best known of all the former students was Dr. John A. Wyeth of New York City. Wyeth had already established a national reputation for himself in two areas. He was one of the leading surgeons in the country at the time. But in the Shoals area he was best known as a historian. Wyeth was a great admirer of General Nathan Bedford Forrest and had written several books and articles about him.

In accord with the well-established tradition of eating at reunions, shortly after the twelve o'clock hour, boxes and baskets of food were brought forth and spread on the ground behind the church "for the convenience and pleasure for all."

As the afternoon waned away, the former students and faculty wandered over Lawrence Hill now covered with saplings and briers. They remembered open streets, fine residences, and college buildings, and longed to see them again.

To that end they adopted a resolution requesting that the Federal Congress reimburse the college trustees $60,000 as payment for the college property destroyed in 1863. But it was not to be. The Yankee-controlled Congress was no more sympathetic than the Yankee army. But the reunion did have a lasting impact. It stimulated a lively interest in LaGrange College and Military Academy that still exists today.

Cotton Fields

In early fall cotton fields are white with fluffy fibers. It has been so for over two hundred years. Cotton has been a major part of Southern life since the arrival of the first settlers. Until rather recently cotton represented wealth. It was the only cash crop farmers had.

The cotton blossom faded in midsummer and cotton bowls grew and burst open in the hot summer sun. Farm families looked forward to weeks of hard labor picking the cotton by hand, stuffing it in a heavy "cotton sack" and at night nursing the sore fingers that had been pricked again and again by the sharp point of the cotton bowls. Less sensitive but more tired after a long day of work was the "aching back" which was bent over all day during the picking period.

Cotton Fields in the Tennessee Valley

After the cotton had been picked it had to be ginned (seed removed). Prior to the Civil War, cotton gins were generally located on the plantations or large farms where the cotton was grown. Many were hand operated. But in the late 19th century ginning became a big business with expensive machinery. Farmers then hauled the cotton in carts, wagons, and later trucks to the nearest modern gin.

As the cotton was ginned, it was pressed into bales usually weighing about 500 lbs each and then sold.

This was a happy time in the life of a farm family. For many families, this was the only time of the year when cash money actually came into the hands of the farm family. Buying clothes, shoes, and many other things that were essential for survival was usually done in October, November, and December. When debts were paid and the necessities of life were purchased, the "cotton money" was soon gone. The typical family could look forward to another year with the assurance of little or no income to supplement the income from the cotton crop.

Hauling Cotton to the Gin

Florentines Dream of Economic Growth

The founders of Florence believed that the city and area would someday be a prosperous, industrial/business center. While lots in and around Florence were being advertised in 1818, the founders often pointed to the natural and man-made opportunities for economic growth of the Shoals area.

In the 1890s this dream seemed to be beyond the reach of mortal man. A major depression swept through the country with serious local consequences. The Florence Boom, which had resulted in a population increase from about 1500 in 1887 to about 7000 in 1892, had come to a halt. Many businesses which had grown up during this boom time had failed; real estate development was at a standstill, and prices of farm products were at rock bottom. The Southern Female University had moved from Florence to Birmingham and the Florence Synodical College was on the verge of collapse. The dream of prosperity was indeed a very dim vision.

But Florentines, like most folk in the Shoals, have a toughness which often turns failure into success. The hardships of the 1890s did hurt the people of the Shoals, but it also stimulated a will to fight back, to work for something better. In those hard times the Lauderdale County Fair was organized, the Bailey Springs University came into existence and several other new ventures became realities.

Two ventures that demonstrate the unity and strength of the Florentines, although ultimately complete failures, deserve some attention.

About 1892 the Alabama Legislature appropriated funds for the establishment of a Girls' Industrial School. The Florence Mayor and Council, with the support of business and professional men, launched a movement to persuade the State leaders to build the school here at Florence. The highlight of this movement came on May 13, 1895, with a mass meeting held in the county courthouse. As was typical of the day, several speakers explained the advantages of locating the school in Florence. Overwhelming support was given to the project. The Trustees of the Florence Female Synodical College led the way by agreeing to turn over their buildings and grounds (located where the main post office is located today) to the city, provided the city would take over a $7000 mortgage. It was believed that these buildings and grounds could be offered as an inducement to locate the school in Florence. Also, a committee was created to raise $2500 to be offered as further inducement. This soliciting committee went to work, and by the evening of the following day most of the needed funds were pledged. With this strong backing from the community, Mr. J. K. Powers, President of the Florence Normal School, and R. T. Simpson, a prominent attorney and legislator, left for Montgomery to present the offer to the State Commission charged with responsibility for selecting the site.

Despite great enthusiasm, the Florence offer was not accepted. The Girls' Industrial School was built at Montevallo and is today known as the University of Montevallo.

One writer claimed that Florence in the 1890s was "low down in a low place and like a drowning man, was ready to grab any kind of floating straw." Another project to help return Florence to prosperity, a project known as "Florence on Wheels" was set in motion. This "wild-goose scheme" was launched by Florence businessmen. According to plans, a train would be chartered. Timber, mineral, and agricultural resources of Lauderdale County and manufactured products (such as the products of Cherry Cotton mill and Florence Wagon Works) were to be carefully exhibited on the train. It would then be sent on a tour throughout the country, especially the northern states.

A project similar to this had been carried out with rather happy results by the Alabama Department of Agriculture a few years earlier. Florentines confidently expected this advertising would lead to increased industrial growth in the Muscle Shoals area. To carry out the project, local citizens were called upon to contribute at least $10,000 and $20,000 if possible. The brother of Georgia Governor Alfred Colquitt was brought to Florence to head up the project, over the objections of some local leaders who thought several local men were better qualified and needed a job. The project never really got off the ground. Within six weeks the money was all gone and "Florence on Wheels" was not rolling.

These two and many other projects have failed over the years. But there have been many successes which keep the dream of economic progress as strong today as it was in 1818.

The Lauderdale County Fair

Late in October 1892, and for ten years thereafter, the citizens of Lauderdale County and the surrounding area enjoyed some exciting times. The Lauderdale County Fair opened its gates, and exhibitors, horsemen, and the general public looked forward each year to a week of fun and excitement.

County and regional agricultural fairs were popular in Alabama before the Civil War. Fairs had been in the Muscle Shoals region but never on an annual basis and never in Lauderdale County. This was a new venture.

In the 1890s while the country was suffering a major depression, the members of the Florence Progressive Club decided to organize and conduct a county fair. Mr. M. B. Shelton, President of the Merchants Bank in Florence, was appointed leader of the project. He joined with A. D. Coffee, J. J. Paulk, W. L. Douglass, H. B. Lee, and other local leaders in organizing the Lauderdale Fair Association. Shelton was President of the Association. Technically, Shelton was merely the leader, but actually he completely dominated the fair activities for nine years.

The Progressive Club never made clear exactly what they hoped to accomplish with a county fair. It seems that their main project was to establish closer relations between the county farmers and the Florence businessmen. President Shelton stated that it was the purpose of the fair to bring the people of the county and city together "in a social way, giving them a chance to talk over the best means of promoting general prosperity." Shelton had high hopes. He claimed that the fair "would give them (the people) an opportunity to absorb progressive ideas." He maintained that "the whole county needs a better system of public schools, a better system of public roads, and also a better knowledge of how to till the land with the best results and keep it up to a high state of fertility." All these and other benefits were looked upon as benefits which would come from a fair.

Financing the fair was a major problem. Hoping the Progressive Club members would follow his example, Shelton contributed fifty dollars to help launch the project. But most other members gave between ten and twenty dollars. Nevertheless Shelton and his colleagues got a lot of value for the money spent.

A sixty-one acre tract of land located one-half mile west of the courthouse was purchased for ten dollars per acre although previously valued for twenty dollars per acre. On this tract of land Mr. Percy Jones, a local surveyor, laid out the fairground and planned a race track at no cost to the Association. Construction began in July 1892. A one-half mile long race track was laid out and completed in ten days. A grandstand, which would seat over 1000 patrons with exhibition booths located under the seats were built. Shortly thereafter a 'judges' stand, stables, livestock pens, floral hall, and other necessary buildings were completed. Exhibitors found the floral hall to be most interesting. The first floor was used to exhibit farm and orchard products while the second floor was "turned over to the ladies for display of their artistic skill in needlework." A telephone and water line was laid and a chert road was built from downtown to the fairground.

Due to public enthusiasm for the project, much of this work was done free. The remainder was done on a bid basis wherein the contractor was paid one-half in cash and the balance in Fair Association Stock.

While entertainment and personal pleasure was never given as a "benefit", it was at the core of the Fair activities. The promise of entertainment, not the agricultural exhibits, pulled in the crowds which averaged 1200 per day. Horse racing was conducted every day along with some especially exotic races. On one occasion, a race was held between a horse and a mule. On another occasion a young man, who had achieved some fame in North Alabama riding a newfangled gadget known as the bicycle, was pitted against a horse. One of the more exciting events was a horse race in which four local women rode horses equipped with side saddles. In this event, Mrs. E. Larrimore won first place while Miss Bessie Steward took second place.

Musical entertainment was always a major attraction. One year the Smithsonia Cornet Band was hired to play at intervals each day. In other years, the Florence Military Band provided the music. The year 1896 was special. On that occasion the band played "The Florence Overture" for the first time before a public audience. Apparently this musical composition was arranged by a local artist and especially for this occasion.

The exhibits were divided into six categories – cattle, horses, sheep, poultry, products of every variety, and "the Ladies Department." Each group had many sub-divisions. Apparently winners in animal exhibits received monetary prizes while winners in the farm products and ladies department received badges recognizing their first and second place standing.

There was always some uncertainty about the monetary prizes. Shelton promised monetary prizes and awards, but perhaps with a banker's appreciation for money, he insisted that all debts must be paid before any monetary prizes should be distributed. He might well have been motivated by the fact that he often had to use his own money to conduct the fair.

Recognizing the importance of food, the ladies of the First Methodist Church were given exclusive rights to sell lunches during the first year of operation. Shelton claimed that the women made more profits than the income he had from the sale of tickets at twenty five cents each. In later years, all major churches were permitted to share in this lucrative activity. Vendors of peanuts, soft drinks, and other such foods were charged a privilege fee.

Apparently the Fair Association skirted on the verge of financial ruin every year, although the Fair was conducted with great success in terms of public interest and attendance for nine years. But unhappiness was growing. Mr. Shelton was accused of being a "dictator" which he later admitted without apology. Horsemen and others wanted larger prizes. In view of the discontent, Shelton resigned.

Mr. J. J. Mitchell, a local attorney, was selected by the Progressive Club to be President of the Lauderdale Fair Association. Mitchell moved quickly to satisfy the malcontents. During the tenth year of operation, prizes were increased and more expensive entertainment was employed. The results were bankruptcy. But the tenth year was not a total failure. Mr. Mitchell used his position to become acquainted with nearly every rural voter in the county. The following year he was elected to the Alabama House of Representatives by a large majority.

Sacred Harp Singing, an American Original

Muscle Shoals has gained national recognition for its music. Sacred Harp Music, an American original, was part of that musical heritage.

The name "Sacred Harp" as a kind of music came into existence in 1844 when B. F. White and E. J. King of Harris County, Georgia, published a song book entitled "The Sacred Harp, a Collections of Psalms and Hymns, Odes and Anthems..." The title of the book gave the name Sacred Harp to the music.

Sacred Harp music is an American original although its roots extend far back into European history. The music was brought to New England in early colonial times. To promote this music, singing schools were organized. These schools, usually lasting two or three weeks in the late summer each year, did much to popularize the music. Song books with performance techniques were published for use in the singing schools.

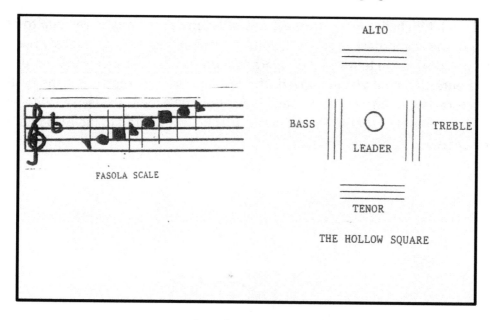

Sacred Harp Singing

Gradually Sacred Harp music spread to the South and West where it gained the strongest hold on the American frontier. Today it has spread throughout the U. S. and is still popular in England.

Sacred Harp music has several unique characteristics. It involves the use of four notes: mi, fa, sol, la. When written on the printed page, each of these notes has a definite shape. The note fa is symbolized by a triangle, sol by a circle, la by a square, and mi by a diamond. Singers sing the notes as well as the words of the songs.

In modern times this music is often dubbed "fasola" singing or shaped note singing. In American song books, the songs are nondenominational. All are closely related to the Christian faith and the American religious folk culture.

At singings, the singers typically arrange themselves in what is known as a Hollow Square. Altos and tenors face each other and the bass and treble face each other. They sing the notes of a song first, followed by the words. In the 19th century, many singers could neither read nor write. They sang by memorizing the words and recognizing the shaped notes. The singing is without any accompanying instruments, although a tuning fork may be used "to keep the singers somewhere between bass and tenor."

Ordinarily, Sacred Harp singers sing for their own pleasure, not to entertain an audience, although large crowds do gather to listen. Members of the audience often participate in the singing, especially the words of the old familiar songs.

The Muscle Shoals area was never a strong center for Sacred Harp music. But it was a common part of life in rural areas through the Great Depression and World War II. Some significant contributions were made to the music by the people of northwest Alabama. Perhaps the two best known contributors to Sacred Harp Music were Seaborn M. Denson (1854-1936) and Thomas J. Denson (1863-1935) of Winston County. The Denson brothers wrote some songs and published a collection of songs in 1935. But they were best known for their Sacred Harp Singing Schools. They traveled all over the South, teaching mainly during July, August, and September. The schools were usually at rural churches and held for young people between the period of crop cultivation and harvest.

In memory of the Denison brothers a monument was erected in 1944 by their friends, co-laborers, and family on the Winston County courthouse lawn in Double Springs. The brothers devoted their lives and talents to composing and teaching Sacred Harp music, which they thought of as American folk music.

The monument also commemorated the one hundredth anniversary of the publication of the book entitled The Sacred Harp, which gave the music its name.

Traditionally the singings were held mainly in rural churches and that is still true today. But it is not unusual for singings to be held in large cities, and on university campuses, etc... For example, the best known singings in this area are held on the

Samford University campus and in the Burritt Museum in Huntsville. While the music is almost unknown in some parts of Alabama, it is a thriving part of Alabama folk life in such areas as Sand Mountain and the Wiregrass Section of southeast Alabama.

A modern-day Sacred Harp singing follows a well-established tradition. As far back as the 19th century, singings were described as "an all day singing with dinner on the ground." The "all day singing" usually started about 9:30 a.m. and ended about 3:00 p.m. with an hour off for "dinner on the ground." In the early days, women would bring out their boxes and baskets of food and spread it on the ground picnic style. In more modern times, most churches have built some kind of long table for the dinner.

Preparation and spreading of food was and still is a serious matter for women of the church. They would often work hard for three or four days preparing food for the occasion. Attendance at the singing usually ranged from one hundred to about six hundred. The quantity and quality of food was always a matter of great concern.

The "all day singing with dinner on the ground" attracted many people who had no connection with Sacred Harp music. Politicians sought votes and others eagerly looked for old friends that had not been seen since the last singing. Many modern singings have a tradition that goes back well over a hundred years. In many communities, going to the singing is much like going to a homecoming. Many people eagerly look forward to seeing relatives and visiting the graves of their loved ones in the cemetery.

The Sacred Harp music, which was so much a part of life in northwest Alabama in the 19th and 20th centuries, is losing ground in our modern way of life. The telephone, radio, television, fast cars, and the internet all open new vistas, while new styles of music make Sacred Harp music seem old and outdated.

Women in the Shoals Area Gain the Vote

Few Alabama women joined the national women's suffrage movement. Muscle Shoals women had never organized a local chapter of the Woman Suffrage Association, but several individual women had participated in the statewide Alabama Suffrage Association. There had never been a strong effort to persuade the Alabama Legislature to give them the right to vote, but they did urge Congress to pass the woman suffrage amendment to the national constitution. This was generally referred to as the Susan B. Anthony amendment.

This proposed amendment had been introduced in the U. S. Congress in 1878 and reintroduced in each session thereafter until its final passage in June, 1919. After passage by the U. S. Congress, the proposed amendment was submitted to the states for ratification. A least 36 of the 48 states had to ratify the amendment for it to become a part of the constitution.

On August 18, 1920, the Tennessee Legislature, by a one vote majority, ratified the proposed woman suffrage amendment and eight days later it became the nineteenth amendment to the U. S. Constitution.

Women of Alabama now could vote. Actually the women in fifteen states already enjoyed full voting rights as a result of a law passed by their state legislatures. In several other states women enjoyed partial voting rights. But the Alabama Legislature had never seriously considered woman suffrage legislation, although some such bills had been introduced.

On about October 11, 1920, the Lauderdale County Board of Registrars, consisting of John H. Anderson, H. B. Lindsey, and T. C. Andrews, began registering voters. For one week the three registrars met in various places in the county and registered voters. Then beginning on October 18th the Board met for a week in the county courthouse to register Florentines and anyone else desiring to register. A steady stream of women and a few men registered in Florence. By the end of the week 1670 new voters had been added to the voter list. Of this number 1435 were women. Of these new women voters, 990 were in Florence and 445 in the county.

As women showed up to vote, several interesting events occurred. In one case three women well over eighty years of age showed up as a group to register.

Women voters had to meet the same requirements as men. Women were not required to pay poll taxes the first year but they did have to give their ages, which many were reluctant to do. The registrars were understanding when "the more mature women" simply registered at forty-five plus. Many of the younger women would admit to twenty-one plus but nothing specific.

Several women in Florence arrived at the courthouse early, determined to be the first registered women voter in Florence. The registrars got around this problem by letting two women, Miss Eva Paulk and Mrs. W. A. Fox, register at exactly the same time immediately after the books were opened. In registering, each woman filled out the required registration application. Then each white woman was immediately issued a certificate authorizing her to vote.

Black women were treated differently. After the State Constitution of 1901 was adopted, black men in Alabama had been completely disfranchised. Now political leaders feared that the woman suffrage amendment would bring on a deluge of black voters, both male and female.

This fear of potential black voters was enhanced when several "colored women" did make application to register to vote in Florence. Apparently no black women registered in other parts of the county. The registrars treated the black women with respect and let them fill out the application. But instead of issuing them a certificate authorizing them to vote, the applications were collected and held until the end of the registering period. At that time a letter was mailed to each black registrant informing them whether they could vote. A total of thirty "colored women" in Florence became voters.

Franklin County, with a population much smaller than Lauderdale, had more women registering to vote. This resulted from local political activities. In Franklin County the Republican and Democratic parties were about equal strength. Leaders in both parties feared the new women voters "may join the wrong party." Hence party members worked diligently to get the women registered and into their party. Apparently the women voters, like most men voters, were about equally divided between the two parties.

Political leaders all over the nation were worried about the impact of women voters. To teach women how to vote and encourage them to vote Democrat, the local leaders organized a public meeting which was attended by a large number of women. Mrs. Mary Inge Hoskins presided. Mrs. Susan K. Vaughn, Mrs. R. E. Meade, Mrs. Emory

Kirkland, and Mrs. James Brock were speakers. At least two men, Mr. S. W. Frierson and Dr. Henry J. Willingham spoke. These men had never worked for women suffrage, but at this meeting they voiced the belief that women in politics would aid in solving many local and national problems.

The presidential election of 1920 was held a few days after the Alabama women registered to vote. Apparently the women nationally and locally followed the men. The Republican Party won the presidential election by a landslide and Warren G. Harding became president. Locally the great majority of votes cast went for the Democrats.

Oscar Stanton DePriest: A Black Florentine in Congress

In 1928 Oscar Stanton DePriest was elected to the United States Congress. He was the first black elected to Congress in the 20th century and the first black elected from a northern state.

His election was significant. At that time most blacks in the south could not vote and had little political influence. The black Americans now had a voice in the highest levels of government.

Oscar Stanton DePriest was born in Florence, Alabama on March 9, 1871, to Alexander R. and Mary (Karsner) DePriest. When Oscar was six, his family moved to Kansas in what was then known as "the Kansas Exodus." After finishing grade school he completed a two year business course at Salina Normal School and soon thereafter moved to Chicago.

Oscar DePriest was a man of intelligence, energy, and ambition. He became very successful in the construction and real estate business which he continued throughout his life.

DePriest was an energetic political organizer. Thousands of blacks were moving out of the South to Chicago. He once set forth very clearly his beliefs about blacks in politics in a statement to his black supporters. "You will never get what you want politically unless you will elect leaders who will fight for your interest... Don't complain about racial discrimination. Change it by practical politics."

DePriest spent much time helping blacks register to vote and to support the Republican Party. In 1904 he was elected to his first public office. For the next forty seven years, he was in and out of public office. In 1915 he was the first black to be elected Chicago City Alderman. DePriest was always a loyal Republican, and an energetic organizer and patronage dispenser with close connections to Chicago Boss William (Big Bill) Thompson.

In 1928 DePriest became the Republican candidate in the Illinois 3rd congressional district which was predominantly black. He won the General Election and took his seat in the 71st Congress in early 1929. He was reelected twice. In 1934 he was defeated by another black man, Arthur W. Mitchell, a Democrat, who had originally lived in Alabama.

The election of DePriest launched a new era. Since that time there has always been a black voice and a black presence in the halls of Congress.

DePriest's service in Congress brought no major successes but it did bring controversy and mixed reactions. His very presence stimulated controversy over the racial barriers to the Congressional Dining Room. National controversy arose when President and Mrs. Herbert Hoover refused to invite Mrs. DePriest to tea with other congressional wives. She was later invited but under restricted circumstances which stimulated more controversy. His presence challenged many established racial barriers.

His congressional activities stimulated a mixed reaction among blacks. He condemned and voted against federal aid to the needy, but tried to prevent government job discrimination in the South. He voted against an anti-lynching bill which would have made lynching a federal crime. But introduced his own bill which would have punished local officials who permitted lynching to go unpunished. It failed to pass. Probably the biggest legislative success was the passage of a bill which prohibited racial discrimination in the Civilian Conservation Corp.

While DePriest's six years in Congress were not capped with great achievements, they did launch a new era in that it started the return of black political power on the national level.

DePriest was always a spokesman for his fellow black Americans. Shortly after arriving in Washington, he spoke in a meeting of the Association for the Advancement of Colored People. In the address he stated that in his youth in Florence, he had witnessed the lynching of three Negroes and that he and his family had been forced to leave the South because Negroes were persecuted and oppressed.

This speech was well received by his black audience, but many Florentines took the remarks as a personal insult and felt that it unfairly degraded Florence and the entire South.

Professor J. P. Dyer, History Professor at Florence State Teachers College, undertook a research project to determine the accuracy of the DePriest statements. In the process he interviewed numerous people of both races about their memory of life in Florence during the time period DePriest was describing.

Dyer found that most people claimed that DePriest could not have seen three Negroes lynched in Florence in the 1870s. It was learned that in 1872 three persons were lynched in Florence but they were white men, not Negroes. Many Florentines pointed out that DePriest was about two years of age at the time and would have no memory of the lynching's.

Many white Florentines also pointed out that DePriest could not have seen a Negro lynched in Florence because the first lynching of a black man in Florence occurred in 1882 after DePriest had moved to Kansas.

There was a widespread feeling that Congressman DePriest had deliberately lied and smeared the good name of Florence and the entire South in order to gain favor with his audience.

Also, many people of Florence claimed that the statements by DePriest that he and his family were forced to leave the South were simply not true. It appeared that the DePriest family was good, honest, hardworking people. They were well respected by their neighbors, black and white. It was generally believed that the DePriest family was not driven out of Florence by any kind of oppression. Many people believed they left because land, jobs, and educational opportunities were greater in Kansas than in Alabama.

Actually, the move of the DePriest family to Kansas was part of a large movement of people to Kansas. In the years after the Civil War, life in the South was hard for all people, especially for former slaves. In the late 1870s thousands of black Americans moved out of Georgia, Alabama, and Mississippi to Kansas. This movement was often referred to as the "Kansas Exodus." This was part of a much larger movement of Black people out of the South which continued for the next hundred years.

It is difficult to speculate with certainty on the motives Congressman DePriest had in making the "insulting statements" about Florence and the South. He was in all probability simply reflecting the view of the audience. Also, creating anger among the southern white Democrats probably enhanced his standing among his black Republican constituency in Chicago.

The Great Depression in the Muscle Shoals Area

In 1931 the Muscle Shoals area, like the rest of the nation, was experiencing what later became commonly known as "Hoover Days." Very few people in the Muscle Shoals area could look back with pleasure on the early 1930s. In 1931 the Florence Chapter of the American Red Cross conducted a survey of families in Florence and Lauderdale County and found that 667 families, consisting of nearly 3500 persons lacked the basic necessities of life. The following year the Community Chest in planning its appeal for funds conducted a "systematic investigation" and discovered that about one-fourth of the population in Florence and the surrounding area were "without work or other means of support." Hundreds of others struggled to get along with part-time employment or by picking up odd jobs here and there.

The surveys showed about fifty percent of the unemployed lived in urban areas and fifty percent lived in Lauderdale County.

Almost without exception the human suffering was blamed on the lack of employment. A few news reports and some public statements hinted that some people were too lazy to work, but most people, especially community leaders, accepted the obvious truth that an adequate number of jobs simply did not exist.

While unemployment or the lack of jobs did constitute a real problem, there were other conditions contributing to the suffering. At least three of these factors should be kept in mind:

1) In the nineteenth century most people were subsistence farmers. Their level of living depended on what and how much they produced on their farm. Most farmers produced mainly crops that could and would be used by their families rather that sold for cash. Hence a lack of jobs did not hurt these folks so badly. But, by the 1930s most of these farmers had become "cash croppers" and depended mainly on their cash income. While many farmers still produced some subsistence crops, they mainly depended on selling their products for cash in order to buy things they needed.

2) Regardless of the crop planted, farmers could sell their crops for practically nothing in the early 1930s. For example, many cotton farmers produced cotton at a cost of 5.5 cents per pound and in 1932 often had to sell it for less than cost. The underlying explanation for this situation was that the nation had a surplus of cotton on hand. In 1932 before the fall harvest, a two year

supply of cotton was already stored in the warehouses of the nation. This same situation was true with many other crops.

3) Finally, there were practically no welfare programs in Alabama in the early 1930s. The federal government gave practically no assistance during these "Hoover Days." The Alabama Welfare Department did exist but had no significant amount of money or a program to lend assistance to unemployed people. The state and local government simply did not have the bureaucratic machinery, the planned programs, or the resources to render effective assistance to those in need.

The more-well-to-do people of the Muscle Shoals area were sensitive to the suffering in their local communities partially because it touched the lives of everyone. At the time there was little complaint about the failure or slowness of government at any level to render assistance. The people of the Shoals area, like the American people, had a heritage of independence, of standing on their own feet, and of taking care of themselves and their families. There was no tradition of government aid. Hence none was really expected.

Yet it was obvious that many families and individuals had lost their ability to support and care for themselves. Private suffering had become a community problem. The people of the Muscle Shoals area rose to the occasion, demonstrating initiative, energy, and human compassion for those in need.

The compassion felt for suffering neighbors took a positive form in the Muscle Shoals area. The local Red Cross was in the forefront of the efforts to meet the needs of those who had inadequate food and clothing. By mid-winter 1931-32 the Red Cross had exhausted its resources but was able to secure an appropriation of $11,000 from the national office of the Red Cross in Washington. It seems that much of the Red Cross assistance was aimed at helping people help themselves. More than $2500 was spent on seed to encourage production of vegetables. They also distributed 240 dozen jars for canning food. Of course some food was distributed to the needy, but clothing and shoes were the main object for distribution, especially in winter.

In March 1932 a group of community leaders came together to consider the problem of relief. They issued a statement claiming that the need for relief "has never been greater than at present." A strong appeal was made throughout Lauderdale County for "money and supplies." Farmers especially were urged to contribute food.

To collect donations and coordinate distributions, the leaders in Florence organized the Florence Good Will Center. Many churches, civic clubs, and individuals made donations through the Good Will Center rather than to individuals.

One of the more interesting activities of the Good Will Center was the establishment of a Community Garden. Mr. C. N. Curry donated the use of 20 acres in McFarland Bottom for growing crops for relief of unemployed people. Numerous people volunteered their labor, while others contributed seeds, tools, fertilizer, and such. The Standard Oil distributor contributed gasoline to operate a tractor.

The efforts did not stop with production. Mrs. A. J. Martin was chairperson of a group of women who took on the job of canning vegetables from the garden.

In the fall of 1932 the campaign for the Presidency between Democratic candidate Franklin D. Roosevelt and the incumbent, Republican Herbert Hoover, was under way. Apparently, contrary to some present day practices, local problems took precedent over national politics. Local leaders were predicting that the winter of 1932-33 would bring forth a larger number of people needing help than ever before. The editor of The Florence Herald claimed that "a grave problem faces us" and "it must be met with sympathetic and courageous action."

The work of the Community Chest was one example of such "courageous action." In the fall of 1932, Mr. Henry A. Bradshaw and Mr. W. H. Mitchell, leaders of the Community Chest, planned an appeal for $12,000. This sum was far larger than that of any previous drive. In 1930 the Community Chest had raised $9300 which was the largest raised up to that time. The leaders proudly announced that only 2.5 percent of their collection was spent on overhead cost. All labor and building space was donated.

The appeal for $12,000 aroused much sympathy and support. One writer admitted that it was difficult to urge fellow citizens to give when it was known that "nearly everyone is laboring under difficulties." But it was pointed out by The Florence Herald that "everyone should reflect on the fact that hundreds of children right in our own midst are without sufficient food and clothing. They eagerly eat stale bread or any scraps of food which they can get to keep their little bodies alive."

Donations came in many forms. All the employees of Rogers Department Store, the Florence Times, and the Coca Cola Bottling Company contributed the earnings from two days of work. In another case, the Community Chest gave food to a needy family which responded by giving the Community Chest a handmade quilt. The Community Chest sold chances on the quilt and raised even more funds.

Despite the magnificent community volunteer effort to help those in need, the task was simply too great in the long run. General poverty in the depression era reduced the ability of people and businesses to give. Also competition between volunteer organizations resulted in a haphazard distribution of the assistance that was available.

But major changes were under way. During the nineteenth century, poverty and hardship was generally looked upon as an individual or family problem. By the 1930s, mass poverty was generally thought of as a community problem. Then, shortly after the election of President Franklin D. Roosevelt in November, 1932, poverty and human suffering due to unemployment began to be seen as a national problem which commanded the attention of national leaders. The development and proliferation of numerous welfare programs at all levels of government became a fact of modern life.

Jesse W. Stutts, Florence Druggist

Dr. Henry Lee Stutts (1873-1963) is one of the best known figures in Lauderdale County history.

His younger brother, Jesse W. Stutts (1875-1960), is far less well-known but nevertheless, a major figure in the history of Florence and Lauderdale County.

Jesse Stutts was born in the northern part of Lauderdale County and attended school there. He attended Florence State Normal College (currently the University of North Alabama). After graduation he taught school and farmed in the Greenhill area for a few years and then enrolled in the Vanderbilt University School of Pharmacy. He graduated from there in 1902.

With a license to practice Pharmacy in Tennessee and Alabama, Stutts established the Stutts Drugstore in Florence. It was located at the corner of Tennessee and Court Street but later moved to other locations.

For several years his advertising slogan was "Get the Habit." His brother, Dr. Henry Stutts, usually wrote prescriptions on a pad with the following statement across the top, "Buy your drugs at Stutts Pharmacy. Get the Habit."

In the early 20th century, with "soft drinks" and ice cream growing in popularity, the soda fountain became a standard part of the drugstore business.

Stutts always liked young people. To attract them to his business, the soda fountain was set up to look like a grape arbor with booths surrounded by grape vines on trellises. Stutts advertising assured the public that his soda fountain served the "fanciest drinks" anywhere and was the "leading ice cream parlor in Florence."

The Stutts drugstore quickly became a social center for the young people. In the beginning of the twenty first century, some of the older Florentines still remembered the Stutts Drugstore. One lady claims that during her teenage years, going to Stutts' soda fountain was the "highlight" of her week. It was "the place" to go. When pressed for what she enjoyed most about the place, she could only remember that it was the only place in downtown Florence with a clean restroom.

Jesse Stutts carried the pharmaceutical business well beyond the retail drug trade. In the early 20th century almost anyone could produce and sell patent medicines. These medicines were advertised widely and were seldom tested to insure safety and effectiveness. Jesse Stutts put his pharmaceutical knowledge to good use and produced several medicines that aimed at solving common health problems. These patent medicines were produced in downtown Florence by the Stutts Laboratories and sold thru the J. W. Stutts Drug Company.

Probably the best known and most popular patent medicine produced by Jesse Stutts was his "Scratch-No-More Liniment." As the name suggests, this medicine was designed to relive discomfort caused by most kinds of itching.

Several other medicines were formulated to provide relief from common health problems in the South. Stutts "Eas-it Liquid", was a formulation intended for the treatment of headaches, neuralgia, nervousness, feverishness, sour stomach, heartburn, periodic pains for women, and several other unpleasant conditions. His "M-S Soap" seems to have been especially good for treating sores, cuts, burns, dandruff, itch, lice, crabs, pimples, and body odor. It was also widely used as "flea soap" for use when washing the family dog. Stutts "G-D" (Germ Death) was used for the treatment of infections in both man and beast while his "Gargleze", an antiseptic, was used for sore throats and bad breath. "We-Ta-Ka Tonic" was used in treating constipation, acid indigestion, etc. Every summer a liquid concoction known as "Stop-the-Heat" was widely used for relief from poison oak and bites from chiggers, mosquitoes, ticks, and other such pests.

Stutts closed the drugstore in 1939 and devoted his time to the production and sale of his patent medicines until his retirement in 1954.

The Stutts brothers, Jesse and Henry, were very creative and always open to new ideas. The brothers joined with E. J. Parker in developing a gadget known as Stutts' Hygienic Fuel Saver. Little information has been found about the gadget. Apparently it was designed to conserve fuel while purifying the air and providing heat. The Stutts Hygienic Fuel Saver was patented in the U. S. and ten European countries.

Jesse W. Stutts married Lull Johnson. Their daughter, Virginia, married Paul Judson Carlton. Virginia and Paul Carlton had one son, Paul Carlton Jr., who was in the insurance business in Florence.

Paul Jr. and other members of the Stutts family recently gave a larger collection of the Stutts family papers to the Archives in the University of North Alabama Library.

Amateur Boxing in the Muscle Shoals Area

In 1940 and 1941 local amateur boxers brought the Alabama Golden Gloves Boxing Team Trophy home to Florence. Along with the team trophy came several individual state championships.

Amateur boxing in the Gold Gloves competition began in Chicago in 1926 and spread gradually throughout the nation. The first Golden Gloves contest in Alabama was held in Birmingham in 1935 under the sponsorship of the <u>Birmingham Age-Herald</u>. Individuals and teams representing towns, clubs, and military units participated in that competition.

Apparently Manuel H. Guerro was the "father of amateur boxing" in the Muscle Shoals area. Guerro came to Florence in the 1920s to help start a cigar making industry. After its failure he joined the Florence Fire Department. In about 1938 he organized the Muscle Shoals Athletic Club and started training interested boys in the art of boxing at the Florence fire station. A short time later he established a gym in the one hundred block of east Tennessee Street. Their equipment was available and free for young men who wanted to develop their boxing talents.

About this same time C. O. McNess, who was in the insurance business in Florence, organized the Florence Athletic Club. These two men, Guerro and McNess, provided leadership and supervision of boxing in the Shoals area. Guerro was basically a trainer while McNess was essentially the business manager and matchmaker.

Guerro made contact with the Golden Glove organization and in 1939 brought that organization to the Shoals area. Amateur boxers from ten northwest Alabama counties and three counties each in Mississippi and Tennessee were invited to come to Florence and participate in the North Alabama District Competition in January 1940. Winners and runners-up in this competition were given an all-expense paid trip to Birmingham to participate in the State Golden Gloves Competition.

In this statewide competition, three Florence fighters including Tony Muro (lightweight), became the state champions in their weight classes. In addition to the individual honors, their success resulted in the State Champion Team Trophy being brought home to Florence.

Florentine leadership in amateur boxing was revealed in another event shortly after the Golden Gloves Competition. In March 1940 the Amateur Athletic Union held its

Southeastern Regional competition in Florence. About 50 boxers from all over the South came to Florence to compete for regional honors. During these contests "Dump" Davenport became the Southeast Regional Lightweight champion. Winners in this competition were authorized to participate in the national finals in Boston. While there was much local interest, the AAU showed no further interest in the Muscle Shoals area. During these competitions, amateur boxers were assigned to one of eight classes according to weight. These classes included: flyweight (under 112 lbs.), bantamweight (112-118 lbs.), featherweight (118-126 lbs.), lightweight (126-135 lbs.), welterweight (135-147 lbs.), middleweight (147-160 lbs.), light heavyweight (160-175 lbs.), and heavyweight (175 and above). Matchmakers preferred to arrange bouts between fighters within a category, but exceptions were often made.

The year 1941 was probably the finest year for amateur boxing in the Muscle Shoals area. Florence was again designated the center for the Northwest Alabama Golden Glove District tournament. In January 1941, fifty-nine fighters from Lauderdale, Colbert, and neighboring counties came to Florence to engage in the elimination bouts. In this district competition there were 17 competitors in the flyweight class, 7 in the bantamweight class, 7 in the featherweight class, 10 in the lightweight class, 15 in the welterweight class, 8 in the middleweight class, 4 in the light heavyweight class, and 2 in the heavyweight class. The winner in each class was given a Golden Glove charm by the Rogers Department Store, a new pair of trunks, and all-expense paid trip to Birmingham to participate in the State Golden Glove tournament.

Again, fighters from Florence met with much success in Birmingham. Aaron Kephart (118 lbs.), Bill Cornelius (135 lbs.), and Worley Alexander (147 lbs.) won the state Championship in their respective weight class, which resulted in Florence being awarded the State Golden Gloves Team Trophy for a second straight year.

In later years several other fighters from the Muscle Shoals area became state Golden Glove Champions. Jack Whitten, Gerald Pitts, Frankie Thompson, and W. R. "Dub" Bevis all became champions in their respective weight categories. Probably many other individuals met with similar success but the record of their achievements has been lost to this writer.

Boxing in these early years before World War II had tremendous appeal among the young men. Jobs were scarce and money always in short supply. The promise of fame and fortune lured many young men into the ring. Nationally, boxing was a popular sport and much was made of the fact that Jack Dempsey fought five fights, each with a purse exceeding one million dollars. In the post-World War II years it was argued that boxing kept kids off the streets at night, reduced drinking and juvenile delinquency, and attracted tourists to the Muscle Shoals area. But in most cases, simple enjoyment of the sport was the real attraction for most young men.

There is no way of knowing how many youngsters put on the gloves and stepped into the ring to do battle in the years before World War II. The following is a partial list of the boxers: Claude Akridge, George Alexander, Paul Anderson, Raymond "Pete" Bevis, Raymond Balentine, J. W. Brewer, Ott Chiriaco, Chandler Crim, Buford Chandler, Earnst Earp, Ernest Hodges, "Buck" Hamilton, O'Neal Harris, Billy Hopkins, "Dump" Davenport, Raymond "Dutch" James, Marin James, Red Keaton, Chuck Kenross, Andy Lewis, Billy Mitchell, Harold Mayes, Curtis McLemore, Charles "Red" Moore, Walter Peden, Billy Pogue, Gerald Pitt, Johnny Rurke Allen Smith, Thurston Tays, J. D. "Buck" Thompson, O. F. Thompson, Louis Vinson, William White, Rudy White, L. L. Whitten, and Hershell Wright.

The United States entered World War II in December 1941. This brought on a new situation. Many young men entered military service and others did not have time for athletics. As a result the Golden Glove competition was discontinued in Alabama in 1942 and did not resume until 1947.

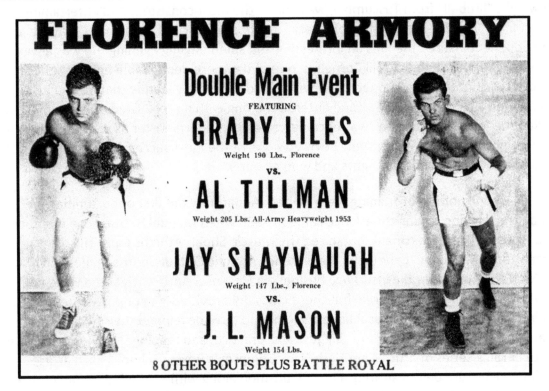

An Evening of Boxing at Fort Willingham (Courtesy of Danny Hendrix)

When boxing was resumed locally after World War II, some of the prewar boxers returned to the ring. But local boxing was dominated by a new and younger crop of amateur fighters. This postwar group included the following: Jack Benson, Jack Boston, David Bratcher, Bobby Beddingfield, David Cornelius, Jerry Cox, Rufus Fisher, Glenn Graham, Buck Hamilton, Martin Hays, Fred Kephart, Grady Liles, Billy McCaig, Milliard Murray, Bimal Poole, Odum Richey, Leon Roberson, Leland Romine, Billy Scarborough, and Rexie Wood.

Many of the boxers were high school students. Some were students at Florence State Teachers College. Some of them came into Florence from surrounding towns and communities. None were professionals although many had such ambitions. Bill Cornelius came close to professional status. He engaged in boxing while in the U. S. Navy and fought a few professional bouts. W. R. "Dub" Bevis fought three professional fights in Birmingham and won all three.

Many of the young men were not really dedicated to boxing and therefore trained and boxed irregularly. But many others were regular in their training and participation. These could be depended on for a good show. Frankie "Buzzsaw" Thompson, the flyweight "fireball" from Tuscumbia, was one of the most consistent and entertaining boxers. His "hell-for-leather style of attack" and unscientific but continuous "flaying" at the opponent insured the fans an interesting and spine tingling evening. He was always popular with the audience. Bill Cornelius, one of the more dependable fighters, once lost a bout to a Birmingham competitor. He explained the loss by stating that he had just completed a ten hour work day and entered the ring with no rest. Grady Liles, sometimes called the "slashing machine" was once described by a sports writer as a "good fighter in any weight category." W. R. "Dub" Bevis was one of the most successful local fighters. He fought a total of 79 amateur fights and won all but 9.

Opportunities for training were limited. Apparently the first opportunities for some training and boxing experience came in 1938 when Manuel H. Guerro, a member of the Florence Fire Department, organized the Muscle Shoals Athletic Club. This organization was later replaced by the Florence Athletic Club under the leadership of C. O. McNess who was in the insurance business in Florence. Apparently there were no professional trainers in the area, but these clubs did provide some opportunities for training and practice. Most local boxers seemed to have developed their skills from watching others and from helpful suggestions, practice, and reading. The Florence Herald in 1941 ran a series of articles entitled, "Jack Dempsey's Boxing School." Each article included a picture demonstrating a boxing position along with a detailed explanation as to how a boxer should attack his opponent and defend himself.

The nearest thing to professional training in the Muscle Shoals area came from Manuel Guerro and Bill Cornelius. Guerro offered training lessons in the late 1930s and after World War II Cornelius taught some boxing classes at the gym in Florence. Charles Hughes, high school athletic coach in Rogersville, helped train some of the boys in that area.

National Guard Armory (Fort Willingham) Built 1937 (Courtesy of Robert Steen)

Boxing was normally thought of as an individual sport, but under the leadership of C. O. McNess it became a team sport in Florence. Beginning in 1940, he assumed the role of general manager and "matchmaker." He organized boxing bouts between local fighters. This stimulated local interest and gave young fighters experience in the ring. More important competition was held between Florence "teams" and similar teams from neighboring cities. Normally a good Florence team consisted of eight local fighters, one in each weight class, to fight individual members of a "visiting team." The fighters on the Florence team varied from week to week depending on who wanted to fight at a given time and the kind of opponent available. For example, in April 1940, a Florence team consisting of "Snuff" Copeland, Jay Cornelius, Pete Bevis, Howard "Mutt" Bonds, Howard Ashley, and "Dump" Davenport travelled to Nashville for a contest there. A short time later a team from Pensacola came to Florence and fought a local team consisting of Bill Cornelius, Aaron Kephard, Frankie Thompson, Harold Hodges, Bill Walker, Louis Hardwick,

Junior "Red" Skaggs, and Junior Kennamore. Competing teams came from about twenty-five different cities in Alabama and surrounding states.

Matchmakers preferred to arrange a boxing program with one bout in each of the weight classes. Hence an evening program normally consisted of eight fights and each fight would be from two to five rounds. "Challenge" or "grudge" matches were often arranged without regard to weight. These bouts were always popular with the audience.

Many boys, especially the young and inexperienced, simply did not fit well into the weight categories. Hence matches were arranged in what became known as "the Chigger Division." Bouts in this division gave "the lads" a "chance to show their wares" and "get some experience" in the "break busting game."

While professional boxing nationally was dominated by black fighters with Joe Louis leading the pack, local boxing, like most other activities in the South, was racially segregated. But cracks began to appear in the racial system after World War II and before racial integration was ordered by the Supreme Court. By 1950 a few bouts were scheduled between blacks but there was no interracial fighting. For example, in 1950 a black fighter named William won a bout with Albert Morris, another black fighter, both of Florence. Another Florentine identified only as "Bearcat" fought and defeated "Steamboat" Johnson from Memphis. Other local black fighters included Robert Irvin and Robert Jackson.

The bouts between black fighters were supplements to the planned program and occurred after the contests between white fighters. Few rules were enforced during these bouts. In reality, the contests became exciting "slugging matches" which provided much entertainment for the audience but little promise of advancement or recognition for the fighters. On some occasions five or six black fighters would enter the ring and gang fight until only one remained standing. These fighters were rewarded by the audience throwing coins into the ring.

The boxing programs were usually held on Friday nights beginning in January after football was over and continuing until late summer. The boxing took place in the National Guard Armory, generally known as Fort Willingham. It was located at the intersection of Tennessee Street and Royal Avenue. The building could seat over 1000 spectators, and it was often filled to capacity. In the prewar days, admission was fifty cents for adults and twenty five cents for children. In 1950 a ringside seat cost $1.50 while general admission was $1.00 and children paid fifty cents.

Income from the sale of tickets was used to pay for all the local expenses of the public performance. Also, when Florence teams travelled to other places for return engagements, the expenses were paid from the proceeds of the gate.

Each boxing program was sponsored by a local group which provided local publicity and shared in the revenue. The National Guard and the U. S. Army sponsored boxing programs as part of their recruiting activities. The American Legion Post #11 was the most consistent sponsor. Their main interest was in community service and raising money for various projects. For example, in June 1941 the American Legion sponsored a public exhibition between local fighters in order to raise money for the Lauderdale County unit of the USO. In 1947 a program was arranged between local boxers to take place in Russellville to help raise funds for the construction of the Veterans of Foreign Wars building. The Florence Coca Cola Bottling Company and other local businesses sometimes sponsored boxing events.

Team competition required several officials. Albert "Red" Cofer and Joe Robb often served as referees while Melvin Lancaster and Roy Collins were timekeepers. Harold Mays was the announcer. At various times Wilson Foote, R. C. Doss, Dr. W. C. Kennedy, Ed Hamm, Harold Seaton, and L. L. Roth served as judges.

Grady Liles Knocks Out His Opponent and Then Falls on Him (Courtesy of Danny Hendrix)

For the young inexperienced boxers, traveling provided numerous opportunities for excitement other than boxing competition. On one occasion while returning from Johnson City, Tennessee, C. O. McNess, who was general manager as well as "matchmaker," arranged for the Florence team to come back through and tour the Chattanooga area including Lookout Mountain. Another group toured the Azelia Trail, the Alabama State Docks, and Bellingraph Gardens on their way to fight a team in Pascagoula, Mississippi. One of the most exciting events occurred when the Florence team boarded an airplane and flew to Atlanta for a match there.

After World War II new competing athletic clubs began to appear in the Muscle Shoals area. A Young Men's Club was formed in Sheffield and an Athletic Club in Rogersville. Similar organizations appeared in Muscle Shoals City, Tuscumbia, and Russellville. None of these boxing organizations enjoyed strong leadership, financial support or wide participation by the young men of these communities. Hence they represented a declining interest in boxing rather than a growth.

By the mid-1950s the era of "fistic fury" in the Muscle Shoals area was rapidly fading. On the national level interest in boxing was declining. Other forms of athletic competition were gaining popularity. Probably the biggest blow to amateur boxing in the Muscle Shoals area came in 1947 with the death of Manuel Guerro and then in the mid-1950s when C. O. McNess moved to Birmingham.

Actually the 1950s was an era of economic prosperity where jobs were fairly plentiful and opportunities for higher education a reality for most young men. And the horrors and brutality of World War II were still vivid in the minds of most people. In this kind of world the sport of boxing seemed to be crude and unappealing.

The Beginning of Libraries in the Shoals

There were few libraries in Alabama in the late 19th century. Between 1890 and 1920 this situation began to change. The groups advocating more and better library services were made up usually of fairly well-educated middle class women who valued libraries for their contribution to education. They also stressed personal enjoyment, development of higher ideals of citizenship, and cultural advancement as advantages offered by libraries.

The leading role in the movement for library services was taken by the Alabama Federation of Women's Clubs and the Alabama Association of Women's Clubs in the 1890s. As other women's organizations were formed they joined in the movement. Few men gave the matter their attention. In 1905 the Alabama Library Association was formed and immediately assumed the leading role in the fight for library services.

The early public libraries were formed with private local groups. In the Muscle Shoals area, the Helen Keller Library and Literary Association in Tuscumbia and the Southern Library Club in Florence were typical. Both these organizations were in existence before the Alabama Federation of Women's Club but both became part of that organization.

In 1892 the Helen Keller Library and Literary Association was formed. Membership cost fifty cents and apparently was open to any interested person. Books and magazines were acquired by purchase and gifts. The library opened in 1893 with 940 books. This number had increased to about two thousand by 1896. In the early years of operation the library was opened for two hours each Saturday morning. Each member served as librarian for a definite term without pay. The very early services were to members only but gradually it was opened to the general public. No tax money was involved in this operation.

The Southern Library Club was organized by a group of Florence women in 1895 in much the same way as the Helen Keller Library. In the early years, the Florence library was supported strictly by contributions, fees, and the labor of unpaid volunteers. Library space and equipment was always a problem. After the library had been opened for a few years and moved several times, the Florence City Council agreed to provide a room in city hall, equipped with book cases, tables and chairs. Occasionally the city contributed small amounts of money for books and other reading materials. In Florence and Tuscumbia, as in the entire state of Alabama, these early libraries were private local ventures for which government assumed no real responsibility.

The year 1907 was very important in library history. Library supporters in cooperation with Dr. Thomas Owen, director of the Alabama Department of Archives and History, launched a campaign to secure the passage of an act providing some state support for library services. The Library Act of 1907 created the Library Extension Division within the Department of Archives and History. This was the beginning of support of public library service by the State of Alabama. The service grew and expanded very slowly.

The Library Act of 1919 opened another new era. This was permissive legislation which enabled counties and municipalities to establish and operate free public libraries with tax revenue under very restricted conditions. County Boards consisting of the Probate Judge, the Superintendent of Education, and three appointed members administered the county library program.

Library services did increase and expand in the 1920s, but the permissive legislation produced only limited results. By 1930 over half the counties of Alabama still had no public libraries.

The early effort to secure adequate libraries was so lacking in unity, vigor, and clearly defined objectives, that it could hardly be called a movement. Strong traditions of individualism, resistance to taxation, the high rate of illiteracy, and greater emphasis on physical – rather than mental – activities were the main obstacles to library progress. But by the end of the 1920s the principle of government responsibility for providing library services was established. Then as today the question was not whether to have public libraries, but what quality of library service Alabamians really wanted and was willing to support.

The Many Faces of Christmas in the Shoals

Today, it is quite common to hear complaints about Christmas being too commercialized with accompanying complaints that we are missing the true meaning of Christmas. When such statements are made, they are soon followed by a desire for an "old fashioned Christmas." Just what is an "old fashioned Christmas"? And is there some mysterious "true meaning of Christmas" that escapes us in ordinary daily life?

Actually, a good argument could be made that each Christmas is primarily a reflection of the major concerns of its time. Will we look back on Christmas of 1992 as the happy occasion when the consumers returned to the market place and began to "spend our way out of the recession"?

If we should glance back about seventy years, we find other pressing concerns. In December 1941 the Japanese bombed Pearl Harbor. For the next four years, the "Christmas spirit" seemed to be matched by a "spirit of patriotism." In 1942 many ads adorned the pages of our local papers, each offering "holiday specials" but also appealing for patriotic actions. For example, the Bootery advertised quality shoes but suggested "Give a war bond for X-mas." Consumers were informed that Sears had "gifts for everyone at Sears' low prices" and then advertised "Remember Pearl Harbor, Buy Bonds and Stamps." The telephone company appeared sacrificial with the reminder that "war takes no holiday" and requested customers to avoid making "greeting calls this year" so that the lines could be free for "vital war business."

While business and patriotism were dominant themes, the Christmas spirit was always evident. The First Methodist Church rendered "The Christmas cantata "Holy Night", while the Tri-Cities Male Chorus presented a Yule program before a packed audience in the Sheffield High School. St. John's Episcopal Church invited all to attend a special Christmas service while the USO held a Christmas Dance for servicemen.

The First National Bank took the high road, predicting that the 1942 Christmas "will be friendlier, more neighborly, because shared troubled and labors have brought us all closer. It is going to be an old fashioned Christmas."

If we look back another seventy years to 1892 for a vision of an "old fashioned Christmas," the view is far less interesting. Churches and community groups did practically nothing toward organizing and conducting worship and community programs. Most businesses simply did not appeal to the Christmas shopper, but some did. One jewelry store claimed to be Santa's headquarters. Another business ad informed the public that "Christmas is coming and Santa Claus has left the choicest gifts at Milner's Drugs." There is little evidence of a serious community-wide concern for a "Christmas Spirit" in 1892.

If we move further back in time to December 1860, there was much excitement in the Shoals area, but not with the "Christmas Spirit" or commercial activity. The clouds of war were darkening. Abe Lincoln had been elected President and Governor A. B. Moore had called for an election of delegates to a convention to consider whether or not Alabama should secede from the Union. The election was held on Christmas Eve, 1860. Strong speeches for the Union and others for secession marked the occasion. Some strong minded individuals tried to settle the national problems with fisticuffs. But in the end, the democratic voting process prevailed. Sidney Cherry Posey in Lauderdale County and John Steele in Franklin County, both strong opponents of secession, were elected to the State Convention.

In the election excitement, the "Christmas Spirit" seems to have been subordinated to other considerations. Complaints were made to the Florence Aldermen that slaves wandered about town without controls, and drunkenness and violence was an ever present danger. As was customary in the pre-Civil War days, the town hired two assistants to help the Constable maintain law and order during the holiday season.

It may appear that the "true Christmas spirit" gets lost as we look further and further back in time. This is not altogether true. Probably, thinking people have always sought guidelines as to how good people should act. In 1692, the members of St. Paul's Church in Baltimore wrestled with this problem and adopted a statement offering advice. The statement reads as follows: "Go placidly amid the noise and haste, and remember what place there may be in silence, as far as possible without surrender. Be on good terms with all persons. Speak your truth quietly and clearly; and listen to others even the dull and ignorant; they too have their story. Avoid loud and aggressive persons; they are vexations to the spirit. If you compare yourself with others, you may become vain and bitter; for always there will be greater and lesser persons than yourself. Enjoy your achievements as well as your plans. Keep interested in your own career, however humble; it is a real possession in the changing forces of our time. Exercise caution in your business affairs; for the world is full of trickery. But let this not blind you to what virtue there is; many persons strive for high ideals; and everywhere life is full of heroism. Be yourself. Especially do not feign affection. Neither be cynical about love for in the face of all aridity and disenchantment it is perennial as the grass. Take kindly the council of the years, gracefully surrendering the things of youth. Nurture strength of spirit to shield you in sudden misfortune. But do not distress yourself with imaginings. Many fears are born of fatigue and loneliness. Beyond a wholesome discipline, be gentle with yourself. You are a child of the universe, no less than the trees and the stars; you have a right to be here. And whether or not it is clear to you, no doubt the universe is unfolding as it should. Therefore, be at peace with God, whatever you conceive Him to be, and whatever your labors and aspirations in the noisy confusion of life, keep peace with your soul. With all its sham, drudgery, and broken dreams, it is still a beautiful world. Be careful. Strive to be happy."

Bibliography

Bernauer, Marianne, *A History of St. Florin,* 1965

Daily, Freda S., *A Heritage to Treasure, A History of the Old Chickasaw Nation of West Colbert, County,* 2004

Daniel, Adrian, *The Formative Period of TVA,* 1973

Garrett, Jill K., *A History of Florence,* Alabama, 1968

Garrett, Jill K., *A History of Lauderdale County,* Alabama

Johnson, Leland R., *Engineers on the Twin Rivers, a History of the U.S. Army Engineers, Nashville District, 1769-1978,* 1978

Keller, Captain Arthur H., *History of Tuscumbia,* 1981

Kitchens, Ben Earl, *Gunboats and Cavalry, The Story of Eastport, Mississippi,* 1985

Lamb, Osie Kyle, *A Study of the Social Development and Social Structure of the Community of Leighton, Alabama,* 1931

Leftwich, Nina, *Two Hundred Years at Muscle Shoals,* 1935

McDonald, William Lindsay, *Civil War Tales of the Tennessee Valley,* 2003

McDonald, William Lindsay, *A Walk Through the Past, People and Places of Florence and Lauderdale County, Alabama,* 1997

Otte, Herman Frederick, *Industrial Opportunity in the Tennessee Valley of Northwestern Alabama,* 1940

Pettus, Ronald and Brenda, *A History of Killen, Alabama,* 2002

Prickard, Kate E., *The Kidnapped and the Ransomed, the recollections of Peter Still and his Wife "Vina",* 1968

Sheridan, Richard C., *Deshler Female Institute, An Example of Female Education in Alabama, 1874 – 1918,* 1986

Srygley, F. W., *Seventy years in Dixie,* 1954

Winn, Joshua Nicholas, *Muscle Shoals Canal, Life with the Canalers,* 1978

The Journal of Muscle Shoals History, Volumes 1 – 18.

Index

205

Bluewater Publications is a multi-faceted publishing company capable of meeting all of your reading and publishing needs. Our two-fold aim is to:

1) Provide the market with educationally enlightening and inspiring research and reading materials.

2) Make the opportunity of being published available to any author and or researcher who desires to be published.

We are passionate about preserving history; whether through the re-publishing of an out-of-print classic, or by publishing the research of historians and genealogists. Bluewater Publications is the Peoples' Choice Publisher.

For company information or information about how you can be published through Bluewater Publications, please visit:

www.BluewaterPublications.com

Also check Amazon.com to purchase any of the books that we publish.

Confidently Preserving Our Past,

Bluewater Publications.com

CPSIA information can be obtained
at www.ICGtesting.com
Printed in the USA
LVHW051339070223
738861LV00005B/225